LONDON STATUES AND MONUMENTS

✧

Margaret Baker

Shire Publications Ltd

ACKNOWLEDGEMENTS
Illustrations are acknowledged as follows: Fiona Spalding Smith, pages 8, 11 (bottom), 22, 33, 36, 38, 40 (top), 57 (bottom) and 100; Times Newspapers Limited, pages 18 (top) and 83; the cover and remaining photographs are by Cadbury Lamb.

Copyright © 1968 and 1992 by Margaret Baker. First published in 1968 as 'Discovering London's Statues and Monuments'. Second edition 1980. Third edition, completely revised, 1992, as 'London Statues and Monuments'. ISBN 0 7478 0162 2.

Printed in Great Britain by C. I. Thomas & Sons (Haverfordwest) Ltd, Press Buildings, Merlins Bridge, Haverfordwest, Dyfed SA61 1XF.

British Library Cataloguing in Publication Data: Baker, Margaret. London Statues and Monuments. — 3rd ed. I. Title. 914.2104858. ISBN 0-7478-0162-2.

Cover: *Sarah Siddons's statue, based on Reynolds's painting of her as 'The Tragic Muse', stands on Paddington Green by the Westway Flyover.*

Title page and below: *The lions below Nelson's Column were added in 1867. The lion model died; Sir Edwin Landseer had to work quickly with a decaying carcass.*

CONTENTS

John Wilkes's statue by James Butler, at the corner of Fetter Lane and New Fetter Lane, has now been deserted by much of the Press, whose freedom he championed.

INTRODUCTION

Some obvious gaps in the ranks have closed since the last edition of this selection of London statues and monuments. Newly on the streets are General Eisenhower, Lord Dowding, Samuel Pepys, John Wilkes and Sir Arthur Harris. Wolfgang Amadeus Mozart and Field Marshal Viscount Alanbrooke are planned to join them in 1992, as is a memorial at Canada Gate to the 1,600,000 Canadians who served with British Forces in two world wars.

Rarely is it too early for enthusiasts to start campaigning for their favoured subject: achieving a statue can be painfully slow. Only recently, nearly fifty years after the event, were serious efforts made to complete commemoration of the Second World War commanders. Of such dawdling, Dr Samuel Johnson declared:

See nations slowly wise, and meanly just,

To buried merit raise the tardy bust ...

Who should be next? Sir John Reith, founder of the BBC, an enduring influence on British life, with a face to stir any sculptor's fingers? For him, Langham Place. Or Nell Gwynne, Londoner extraordinary, born in Drury Lane, mistress of Charles II, instigator of Chelsea Hospital? John Evelyn tells how the former orange seller chatted with the king over her garden wall at 79 Pall Mall as he strolled in the park with his dogs. Sir Christopher Wren? London has changed but he would still recognise St Paul's, Greenwich Hospital and his churches. And, if we can have (the austere might say *must* have) fictional Peter Pan, why not fictional Sherlock Holmes, with Dr Watson in attendance? A duo for Baker Street. Our four-footed nominee would be 'Burmese', the Royal Canadian Mounted Police horse that carried the Queen at Trooping the Colour. There is good grazing in St James's Park.

Autumn and winter are prime seasons for statue viewing. Trees are bare, streets less crowded, bronze and stone look well in chill damp air, winter melancholy and a low light, with a backdrop of gulls' wings on the Thames. Those seeking an easy insight into the history of capital and country need look no further than the statues and monuments of London.

The Margaret MacDonald memorial, Lincoln's Inn Fields.

Le Sueur, the sculptor's name, is on the left forefoot of Charles I's stallion near Trafalgar Square. It was cast in 1633, hidden during the Commonwealth and re-erected in 1660 for the Restoration of the Monarchy.

» 1 «
CHARING CROSS, TRAFALGAR SQUARE, LEICESTER SQUARE

At Charing Cross, an irregular open space at the end of the Strand and to the south of Trafalgar Square and the hub of London, an **Eleanor Cross** was erected by Edward I in 1291 to mark the last resting-place of the body of his queen, Eleanor of Castile, on its way from Lincolnshire to burial at Westminster. The cross was removed by Parliament in 1647 as an idolatrous object and its site is now occupied by the statue of Charles I. The Eleanor Cross now to be seen in the courtyard of Charing Cross station is a Victorian replica which was erected in 1863 by the London, Chatham and Dover Railway Company: the architect was Edward Middleton Barry, third son of the architect of the Houses of Parliament, Sir Charles Barry, and the sculptor was Thomas Earp.

The statue of **Charles I** by the Huguenot sculptor Hubert le Sueur was cast in 1633. The statue has a romantic history. It was removed during the Commonwealth and sold to a brazier named Rivett to be melted down. He sold knives and other souvenirs supposedly from the metal but actually hid the statue in his garden and produced it for triumphal re-erection at the Restoration in 1660, and for this happy occasion the poet Waller wrote:

That the First Charles does here in
  triumph ride:
See his son reign, where he a martyr
  died;

And people pay that reverence, as they
  pass
(Which then he wanted) to the sacred
  brass;
Is not the effect of gratitude alone
To which we owe the statue and the
  stone.
But heaven this lasting monument has
  wrought,
That mortals may eternally be taught,
Rebellion, though successful, is but
  vain:
And kings, so killed, rise conquerors
  again.
This truth the royal image does pro-
  claim,
Loud as the trumpet of surviving fame.

Although only 5 feet 4 inches tall, the king would obviously have liked to be taller, for the specification for the statue ran: 'the figure of his Maj. King Charles proportion-able full six feet' — and so it was made.

During the Second World War the statue was moved for safety to Mentmore, Buckinghamshire, and in 1947 was put up again with a new sword in the king's hand. The first sword is said to have disappeared in 1867 when a newspaper reporter climbed on the statue for a better view of a procession and grabbed the sword to steady himself. It fell amongst the crowd and was never seen again. The armour the king is shown wearing is in the collection at the

From Nelson's hat to the pavement at the foot of his Column is 170 feet 2 inches, the distance from Victory's main masthead to the quarter-deck.

Tower of London. The pedestal appears to be the work of Gibbons or perhaps of Joshua Marshall, Architect to the Crown, and the sculptor's name can be seen on one of the horse's hooves. On 30th January each year, the anniversary of the king's execution, the Royal Stuart Society holds a wreath-laying ceremony here which starts at 11 am.

Sir Robert Peel extravagantly described Trafalgar Square as 'the finest site in Europe' and it was laid out in 1829-41 to the design of Sir Charles Barry to commemorate Lord Nelson's victory at the battle of Trafalgar on 21st October 1805. The fluted Corinthian column, one of the best-known monuments in the world, is surmounted by a statue of **Horatio, Viscount Nelson, Duke of Bronte** (1758-1805), which is 17 feet 4¹/₂ inches high and is by E. H. Baily. If it could be seen more clearly it would probably be hailed as a masterpiece. The column itself, of Devon granite and designed by William Railton, is a copy of one of those at the temple of Mars Ultor in Rome and the total height is 170 feet 2 inches. The bronze capital was cast from the cannon of the *Royal George*, which sank at Spithead in 1782 when heeled over for examination of her underwater timbers. Admiral Richard Kempenfelt and many hundreds of her crew were drowned.

At the base of the column are four 20 foot bronze lions by Sir Edwin Landseer, which were added in 1867, and reliefs made from French cannon captured at the battles of St Vincent, the Nile, Copenhagen and Trafalgar: they are the work of the sculptors Watson, Woodington, Ternouth and Carew (who made the one depicting Nelson's death). Annually on the anniversary of the battle of Trafalgar wreaths are laid at the base of the column, including those from the modern ships of the fleet. At the four corners of the square are octagonal lamps set on plinths which are said to be the oil lamps from Nelson's flagship *Victory*, although this is uncertain. In the days of lamplighters they were known as the 'battle lamps' and the men received extra wages for cleaning them, so this provenance may be the true one. The monument cost £50,000 in all, of which £20,000 was raised by public subscription and the remainder voted by Parliament. It is known that a few days before the statue was erected in 1843 fourteen people ate a precarious rump steak dinner on the top of the column. This monument to England's perennial folk-hero is often hidden behind wheeling flocks of pigeons and starlings.

Other statues in the square include that of **Sir Henry Havelock** (1795-1857), who won world-wide renown in the Indian Mutiny, captured Cawnpore and relieved Lucknow.

George IV chose to be depicted in Roman dress, riding bareback and without stirrups.

The statue (1861), the first ever to be made from a photograph, is by William Behnes (1795-1864), whose work was perceptive and noted for its absence of affectation but whose personal habits were so eccentric that the Royal Academy refused to elect him. He died in the Middlesex Hospital after a fall in the street.

Sir Charles James Napier (1782-1853) is by George Cannon Adams, 1855. Napier was a British general and statesman who fought in the Irish Rebellion of 1798, at Corunna in 1808, at Chesapeake in 1813, and later in India. He is holding a scroll and a sword. The plinth records that the most numerous contributors to the fund to erect the statue were private soldiers, so Napier seems to have been a popular commanding officer, perhaps because of his sense of humour. After the battle of Hyderabad in 1843 he sent a despatch with the single Latin word 'Peccavi' ('I have sinned') — Sind then being a part of India.

At the north-east corner of the square is an equestrian statue of **George IV**, 1843, by Sir Francis Legatt Chantrey (1781-1841). For this work Chantrey was to receive £9,000, of which the king paid a third from his own pocket, but at the time of the sculptor's death a large sum was still outstanding and was extracted only with some difficulty from the Commissioners of Woods and Forests by his executors. The statue, which had at first been intended to adorn the Marble Arch, was thus not erected until 1843. George selected the theatrical pose himself (in which he is shown in Roman dress riding bareback without

The busts of three naval commanders face Nelson's column from the north side of Trafalgar Square. From left to right: Admiral Jellicoe, who defeated the German High Seas Fleet at Jutland in 1916; Admiral Beatty, who accepted the surrender of the German Grand Fleet in 1918;

stirrups) and generally seems to have been something of an exhibitionist. A neat story is told of how he was once boasting to the Duke of Wellington of an equestrian exploit on the precipitous Devil's Dyke on the South Downs near Brighton. The king said: 'I once galloped down there at the head of my regiment.' '*Very* steep, Sir', replied the Duke.

Look, too, at the bronze bust, erected in 1948, of **John Rushworth, Earl Jellicoe** (1859-1935), the British admiral, by William Macmillan RA (born 1887), an eminent Scottish sculptor from Aberdeen, who also designed the Victory Medal. Jellicoe is especially remembered for his command of the Grand Fleet in the First World War and for his part in the battle of Jutland in 1916. Two other British admirals

are remembered here. The bust of **David, 1st Earl Beatty** (1871-1936), who accepted the surrender of the German Grand Fleet at Scapa Flow in 1918, is by Sir Charles Wheeler PRA. To these nautical monuments was added in 1967 a bust by Franta Belsky of **Admiral Lord Cunningham (1st Baron Cunningham of Hyndhope)** (1883-1962), noted for his brilliant aggressive strategy in naval warfare in the Second World War.

In front of the National Gallery is a bronze statue, again in Roman dress, of **James II** (1633-1701), king of England and second surviving son of Charles I. He was overthrown in 1688 by William of Orange, two years after the statue's erection. It has had a mobile past for it was first erected in Priory Gardens, removed to the centre of White-

Admiral Cunningham, who sank the Italian ships Zara, Pola and Fiume at the battle of Cape Matapan without any British casualties.

In St Martin's Place, on an island by the National Portrait Gallery, is a monument (1920) by Sir George Frampton (1860-1928) to **Nurse Edith Cavell** (1865-1915), who was shot at Brussels by the Germans in 1915 for alleged spying and assisting the escape of British prisoners of the Germans. To many English minds the execution of Miss Cavell was judicial murder. British tribunals throughout the First World War avoided passing the death sentence on women even for the most serious cases of espionage. Her famous words 'Patriotism is not enough' were added to the monument in 1924 four years after its unveiling by Queen Alexandra. The *Dictionary of National Biography* calls the statue 'one of

Below: *The original of Houdon's Washington is in Virginia, USA. This copy stands outside the National Gallery.*

hall, later to the forecourt of the Admiralty and then to its present site. Many regard this statue by Grinling Gibbons as a superior work to le Sueur's statue of Charles I and it is a strong claimant to the title of the finest outdoor statue in London. Gibbons received £300 for his work and the commissioner and donor was Tobias Rustat, Yeoman of the Robes, who also paid for the statues of Charles II at Windsor and Chelsea Hospital.

The bronze copy of Jean Antoine Houdon's distinguished marble statue at Richmond, Virginia, to **George Washington** (1732-99), first President of the United States (to execute which the sculptor visited America in 1785), was presented by the State of Virginia in 1921 and stands in front of the National Gallery.

Frampton's most conspicuous failures'.

On the north side of the National Portrait Gallery, facing up Charing Cross Road, is a statue by Sir Thomas Brock, 1910, of **Sir Henry Irving** (1838-1905), the actor-manager. Irving rose to fame in 1874 when he played Hamlet for 200 nights and quickly increased his reputation, often with Ellen Terry as his leading lady. He was the outstanding theatrical personality of his day, with a dominant magnetism, a passionate and intense, rather than resonant voice, and was the first actor to be knighted (an honour he resisted for twelve years).

Irving Street leads to Leicester Square,

Above: *Edith Cavell, revered by the British public for her courage and patriotism, was shot by the Germans in 1915 for alleged espionage. Many considered this an act of judicial murder.*

Right: *One of the few theatrical statues in London is Sir Henry Irving, by the National Portrait Gallery. Irving unveiled the statue of Sarah Siddons featured on the cover of this book.*

which takes its name from Leicester House, once called a 'pouting place for princes' for in 1718 George II, when Prince of Wales, moved there after quarrelling with his father, George I, and in 1741 his son, Frederick, Prince of Wales, did the same. To show his opinion of his father Frederick set up a statue here of his *grandfather* which was gilded and usually called the 'golden man and horse'. It gradually decayed and final degradation came when on one night of jollification it was painted in dapples like a rocking-horse. The square is now an ornamental garden and was laid out in 1874 by Albert Grant, the company promoter, at a cost of £28,000. It was refurbished in 1990-2. In the centre is a marble statue of **William Shakespeare** (1564-1616) by Knowles (a copy of the one by Scheemakers in Westminster Abbey) and at the four corner gates to the square are the busts of **Sir Joshua Reynolds** (1723-92) by Weekes, **William Hogarth** (1697-1764) by Joseph Durham, **Sir Isaac Newton** (1642-1727) by Calder Marshall and **William Hunter** (1718-83) by Woolner. All were associated with the square by residence or otherwise.

Also here, in the centre of the entertainment industry, stands a statue of **Charles Spencer Chaplin** (1889-1977), the film actor and comedian, who was born in London. Discovered by Mack Sennet about 1913, Charlie Chaplin soon became famous for his 'little man' character, whose baggy trousers, bowler hat, cane and little moustache the statue, by John Doubleday, and unveiled by Sir Ralph Richardson in 1981, faithfully portrays.

Left: *Joseph Durham's William Hogarth, painter, caricaturist and engraver, is in Leicester Square.*

Below: *Charlie Chaplin's statue stands in Leicester Square's cinema area, facing Shakespeare.*

Above left: *In Whitehall is the 2nd Duke of Cambridge, whose horse was shot under him at Inkerman. As Commander-in-Chief of the British Army for 39 years, he resisted all military reform until forcibly retired.*

Above right: *Horsemen criticise the pose of Earl Haig's horse in Whitehall.*

Below: *This bedragoned mortar, abandoned by the besiegers of Cadiz during the Peninsular War, was the gift of the Spanish government. It stands in Horse Guards Parade.*

» 2 «
WHITEHALL

Whitehall leads from Trafalgar Square to Westminster. In the roadway, opposite the former War Office, is an equestrian statue of the **2nd Duke of Cambridge** (1819-1904) by Adrian Jones. The Duke was Commander-in-Chief of the British Army from 1856 to 1895 and first cousin to Queen Victoria and he is here shown in field marshal's uniform with plumes and whiskers flying and riding a strapping horse. He married the actress Louise Farebrother and their children took the name of Fitz-George.

Between the War Office and the Banqueting House is a statue of the **8th Duke of Devonshire** (1833-1908) by H. Hampton, 1910. The Duke became Minister of War in 1882 and was partly responsible for sending General Gordon to Khartoum and for the failure to rescue him from the siege of the city. He is more pleasantly remembered as a generous landlord and benefactor and as an intimate friend of Edward VII, who often stayed with him.

Through the Horse Guards archway is Horse Guards Parade, the largest 'clear' space in London and the scene of that military exercise, Trooping the Colour, on the sovereign's official birthday. Here are statues of four military commanders. **Garnet Joseph, 1st Viscount Wolseley** (1833-1913) served in the Indian Mutiny and Crimea and commanded the expedition that attempted to relieve Gordon at Khartoum. He was the prototype of Gilbert's 'Modern Major-General' in *The Pirates of Penzance* and Commander-in-Chief of the British

Army from 1895 to 1900. The equestrian statue is by Sir William Goscombe John (1860-1953), a distinguished late Victorian sculptor. When Sir Garnet was winning his victories in Egypt the Army phrase 'All Sir Garnet!' came into common use, meaning that everything was going as it should.

The equestrian statue of **Frederick Sleigh, 1st Earl Roberts of Kandahar and Waterford VC** (1832-1914), is by Harry Bates — one of the two statues of the Earl made by this sculptor. This is a smaller copy of one erected in Calcutta. Roberts commanded the British troops in the Boer War and in 1901 followed Wolseley as Commander-in-Chief. He died at St Omer, France, at the beginning of the First World War after catching a chill.

Nearby is the cast-iron **Cadiz Memorial**, given by the Spanish government to commemorate the raising of the siege of the city in 1812 by the victories of the Duke of Wellington and his troops.

On the south side of Horse Guards Parade is a statue of **Horatio Herbert, 1st Earl Kitchener of Khartoum and of Brooke in Kent** (1850-1916), by John Tweed, 1926. Kitchener fought in the Sudan and Egypt and in the Boer War, becoming Minister of War at the outbreak of the First World War and reorganising the British Army on the basis of voluntary recruiting. After the blunders of the Dardanelles campaign he fell from favour and died when the cruiser *Hampshire* was sunk by the Germans in 1916. Some of his troubles were self-created for he was noted for his arrogance and unwillingness to be advised. The 9 foot 5 inch bronze statue by Franta Belsky of **Lord Mountbatten of Burma** (1900-79) stands on a wide stepped plinth on Foreign Office Green overlooking Horse Guards from the south. It shows him in the uniform of an Admiral of the Fleet and was unveiled by Queen Elizabeth II on 2nd November 1983. The Earl was murdered by the IRA while on his boat near his holiday home in Ireland in August 1979. Sharing Monty's knack of winning the hearts of his troops, Mountbatten was an outstanding figure in the conduct of the Second World War, Chief of Combined Operations (1941-3), then Supreme Allied Commander in South East Asia (1943-6), when the British retook Burma. Appointed Viceroy of India in 1947 and Governor-General 1947-8, he supervised the transfer of power from Britain to India and Pakistan. He was created

Viscount in 1946 and Earl in 1947. In 1947 he returned to his naval career and in 1955 became First Sea Lord and in 1959-65 Chief of the Defence Staff. 'Dickie' Mountbatten, a grandson of Queen Victoria, was in pre-war years a handsome and dashing naval captain and socialite, as well as a later statesman, admiral and socialist. He was not without his critics but his achievements were great. In all these he was ably complemented by his wife Edwina, almost as famous in her own field of welfare and relief work as her husband was in his.

Back in Whitehall, a little further down towards Westminster is the Banqueting House of Old Whitehall Palace. Above the entrance is a lead bust of **Charles I** (1600-49) dating from about 1800. It was through a window of the hall (the precise one cannot now be identified) that the king stepped to his execution on a January morning in 1649, first handing his George (the Order of the

Facing page: *Each November a national Service of Remembrance is held at the Cenotaph in Whitehall, when wreaths of poppies are laid all around it.*

Below: *Mountbatten's statue, by the Czech Franta Belsky, is in Horse Guards.*

Garter whose jewel shows St George) to the Bishop of London with the enigmatic word 'Remember'. There has always been great controversy about the precise spot of the execution. Disraeli was once asked by a supporter for a word of advice for his son. 'Never ask', he replied, 'who wrote the *Letters of Junius* or on which side of Whitehall Charles I was beheaded. For if you do, you will be considered a bore...' About 30th January, the anniversary of the execution, the Society of King Charles the Martyr holds a service of dedication and wreath-laying here.

Opposite the Banqueting Hall is an equestrian statue of **Douglas, 1st Earl Haig** (1861-1928), who commanded the British forces in 1915 during the First World War but has since been denigrated for his mismanagement of the battle of Passchendaele and was attacked by Lloyd George in his *Memoirs*, 1934. He was first president of the British Legion. When the statue, by A. F. Hardiman, was erected in 1937 the knowledgeable were quick to point out that the hind legs of the horse suggested not propulsion but urination. The wretched sculptor was presumably ignorant of such equine habits.

In the lawn facing Whitehall and near the spot where he was beheaded in 1618 is a diminutive statue of **Sir Walter Raleigh** (1552-1618), the Elizabethan courtier, poet and explorer, by William Macmillan RA, erected in 1959 and donated by Anglo-American interests. It was unveiled by John Hay Whitney, the American Ambassador. Raleigh showed admirable *sang-froid* on the scaffold for he poised the execution axe on his thumb to test its sharpness, remarking: 'This is a sharp medicine but it will cure all diseases.' Today Walter Raleigh is best remembered for his promotion of potatoes

Oscar Nemon, sculptor of the statue of 'Monty' on Raleigh Green, is here seen with the plaster cast of his statue prior to the erection of the finished work.

Montgomery, the 'Victor of Alamein', is backed by the Ministry of Defence in Whitehall.

— and of tobacco. He even told Elizabeth I that he could weigh the smoke. The National Society of Non-Smokers is reputed to have attended the unveiling of Raleigh's statue, handing out leaflets bearing the slogan 'Don't make an ash of yourself'. Raleigh, however, may not be long for Whitehall. In 1992 the Department of the Environment announced plans to move him elsewhere, perhaps to his old home, Sherborne Castle in Dorset.

On the same lawn, at present still called Raleigh Green, and appropriately in front of the Ministry of Defence, is a small spare figure, in battledress with the famous two-badged beret, the statue of **Viscount Montgomery of Alamein** (1887-1976), sculpted by Oscar Nemon. During 1979 over £30,000 was raised by public subscription, much of it from men who had served under 'Monty' during the North African campaign in the Second World War. The simple inscription, 'Monty', conveys something of the great affection his troops felt for Field Marshal Montgomery. On the night of the field marshal's death, Sir Brian Horrocks, who as commander of the 13th Corps in North Africa held part of the El Alamein line against the German Afrika Korps, broadcast an obituary. 'A showman, difficult, autocratic — yes, *all* these! But can any other general equal his achievements ... he was the greatest British general since Wellington ... with the passing away of the Victor of Alamein Britain has lost one of her really great soldiers.' The *Daily Mirror* had the final word: 'His troops loved him and he won battles. Could any better tribute be paid to any general?'

In 1944-6 Monty commanded British forces in France and Germany and accepted the German surrender at Luneburg Heath in 1945. After the war his posts included

Deputy-Supreme Commander Europe (NATO) 1951-8, but he will be for ever associated with the 8th Army (Desert Rats) and their victories from Egypt to Tunis. The extraordinary sense of comradeship that marked the 8th Army was strong at the Desert Rats' annual reunions (especially when the field marshal was still alive) and so redolent of the sense of common endeavour of those distant days in the desert that contingents of ex-Afrika Korps members asked if they too could attend to enjoy the nostalgia and memories of that most distinctive of battlefields.

Here too on Raleigh Green is a statue to another Second World War hero, **Field Marshal the Viscount Slim** (1891-1970),

Ivor Roberts-Jones's portrayal of Field Marshal Slim in Whitehall shows him with binoculars, a popular accessory in recent military statues.

Above: *The statue of James II in Roman dress was erected only two years before he was overthrown by William III. It stood in three other locations before being set up here, outside the National Gallery.*

Facing page: *William Shakespeare contemplates the night life of Leicester Square from his vantage point in the 'Shakespeare Enclosure', laid out in 1874 by Alfred Grant MP.*

who led the 14th Army from 1943 to 1945 and fought a memorable campaign to recapture Burma from the Japanese. The statue by Ivor Roberts-Jones shows Slim in battledress and slouch hat and holding binoculars. After his campaign with the 14th Army Slim was Commander Allied Land Forces SEAC and succeeded Montgomery as Chief of the Imperial General Staff, 1948-52. From 1953 to 1960 he was Governor-General of Australia. Around the statue's plinth are the names of battles Slim fought from Rangoon to the Chindwin.

In Whitehall the **Cenotaph** commemorates the dead of the First and Second World Wars and was designed by Sir Edwin Lutyens. It was first constructed in plaster as a saluting base for the Victory March of 19th July 1919 and later rebuilt in Portland stone and unveiled on Armistice Day, 11th November, 1920: the additional inscription to commemorate the fallen of the Second World War was unveiled in 1946 by George VI. On the Sunday nearest to 11th November each year a Service of Remembrance is held which is attended by the monarch, statesmen, the diplomatic corps and representatives of the armed services.

King Charles Street leads from Whitehall to the steps to Horse Guards Road. At the top of the steps is John Tweed's delightful statue (1916) of **Robert, 1st Baron Clive of Bengal** (1725-74). It has three reliefs showing Clive at Plassey, at the Siege of Arcot and reading the Grant of Bengal from the Rajah. After a problem childhood this restless, suicidal but brilliant soldier went to India with the East India Company and founded there the British Empire which was to last for nearly 200 years. Arcot was called 'the turning-point in the Eastern career of the English'. In 1753 Clive returned home with a personal fortune but squandered it and returned to India to become Governor of Bengal from 1757 till 1760. He became Baron Clive in the Irish peerage in 1762 and two years later was back in Bengal reorganising the administration and eliminating corruption but about this time a campaign was begun against him and, although a Parliamentary enquiry exonerated him, his health was broken, he took to opium and ultimately committed suicide.

Robert, 1st Baron Clive of Bengal, was a brilliant soldier. The reliefs on his statue by Tweed illustrate three of his triumphs.

» 3 «
WESTMINSTER

The Houses of Parliament, built 1840-50 by Sir Charles Barry, have a long river frontage decorated with statues and royal arms of **British sovereigns from William the Conqueror to Queen Victoria** and a shorter north front with figures of **pre-Conquest sovereigns**. The sculptor was John Thomas (1813-62), whom Sir Charles Barry found working in a stonemason's yard and put to work adorning his creation. Many of the statues have since been replaced.

In New Palace Yard, Westminster, is a fountain celebrating the **Queen's Silver Jubilee**, by the Polish sculptor Valenty Pyrel. This original piece, of galvanised steel strips painted black, has a series of animals surmounted by St Stephen's crown and representing Europe (unicorn), Africa (lion), America (eagle), Asia (tiger), Australia (kangaroo) and Antarctica (penguin). The fountain, which revolves, was unveiled by Queen Elizabeth II on 4th May 1977.

Parliament Square, laid out by Barry to set off his new buildings, was most successfully re-arranged in the 1960s. The central island contains a group of interesting statues including that of **Benjamin Disraeli, 1st Earl of Beaconsfield** (1804-81), Conservative statesman, man of letters, favourite of Victoria. The statue is by Raggi, 1883. Twice Prime Minister, three times Chancellor of the Exchequer, Disraeli was a meteoric and colourful figure in nineteenth-century British politics and reorganiser of the Conservative party on modern lines. His dash was coupled with foresight for in

1875 he purchased (on his own authority) £4,000,000 worth of shares in the Suez Canal from the Khedive of Egypt and thus secured power and wealth for Britain. Victoria was extremely susceptible to his charm and included his allegedly favourite flower — the primrose — in her funeral wreath. Each 19th April, Primrose Day, the statue is decorated with wreaths of the same flower. Disraeli was nobody's fool and understood the value of his talents, once saying: 'You have heard me accused of being a flatterer. It is true. I *am* a flatterer. I have found it very useful. Everyone likes flattery: and when it comes to royalty you should lay it on with a trowel.'

The **14th Earl of Derby** (1799-1869), a dull but worthy statesman and, with Disraeli, reorganiser of the Tory party, has a statue by Matthew Noble (1874) with panels showing his inauguration as Chancellor of Oxford University. Look at the plinth to see what St Stephen's Chapel, the meeting-place of the House of Commons before 1834, looked like.

On the corner of the square and half-facing the House of Commons is a statue of **Sir Winston Spencer Churchill** (1874-1965), one of the best known statues in London. Churchill was a many-faceted personality but he is best remembered as Britain's wartime Prime Minister and it is this aspect that Ivor Roberts-Jones expressed in his 12 foot bronze statue, unveiled by Lady Spencer Churchill in 1973. The bareheaded figure, in buttoned-up military over-

Appropriately, Sir Winston Churchill's statue in Parliament Square faces the House of Commons.

The statue of Disraeli in Parliament Square was unveiled in 1883. The event was recorded in the Illustrated London News.

coat and grasping a walking stick, reflects an indomitable personality.

Winston Churchill had already had an exciting career as a soldier under Kitchener and as a war correspondent in the Boer War when he moved to politics, first as a Conservative, then as a Liberal (holding a number of high offices) and again as a Conservative, being Chancellor of the Exchequer 1924-9. Although out of office in 1930-8, he spoke repeatedly of the dangers of appeasing the Nazis and of Britain's unpreparedness to deal with aggression. In May 1940 he became Prime Minister; his own comment on that day was: 'I felt as if I were walking with destiny.' He was to remain Prime Minister until his defeat by the Labour party in 1945. His courageous independence of thought, perhaps a handicap in earlier years, came into its own in wartime days and Churchill became an international leader, radiating hope to the enemy-occupied world and expressing the British people's determination to beat Hitler. He was the outstanding orator of the twentieth century.

In 1945 Churchill moved to 28 Hyde Park Gate, his home for the rest of his life. In 1946 he toured the United States (making, among others, his 'iron curtain' speech). He was Conservative Prime Minister again in 1951-5, resigned through ill-health and died in 1965. He is buried at Bladon, Oxfordshire, near Blenheim Palace, where he was born.

His works *The Second World War* (1948-51) and *The History of the English Speaking Peoples* (1956-8) confirmed his literary stature. He received the Nobel Prize for Literature in 1953 and, a talented painter, was made a Royal Academician Extraordinary in 1948. In 1963 he received honorary American citizenship.

The exciting though discordant statue of the South African soldier and statesman **Field Marshal Jan Christian Smuts** (1870-1950) is by Jacob Epstein and is an interesting example of this sculptor's representational work, erected in 1956.

Also on the paved walk is **Henry Temple, 3rd Viscount Palmerston** (1784-1865), by Thomas Woolner, a statue erected in 1876. Palmerston personified Victorian self-confidence at its peak, and although he was accused of 'jingoism' (warlike patriotism) his bluff, adventurous foreign policy protected Britain's interests overseas and built up her prestige. Much of his success came from sheer hard work. An omnibus driver who regularly drove up Piccadilly would point out to his passengers Palmerston's head bent late over the desk at his window, with the words: "E earns 'is wages: I never comes by without seein' 'im 'ard at it.' This statue has unusual merit, for Sir Desmond MacCarthy wrote: 'It ought to be an object of pilgrimage to all the tailors in England. The frockcoat fits like a glove, and though the trousers do not break on the instep enough to suit modern taste, the hang of them is magnificent.' Palmerston kept his diplomatic wit to the end: on his deathbed he was joking: 'Die, my dear doctor? That is the *last* thing I shall do.'

Facing the Houses of Parliament is a statue of **Sir Robert Peel** (1788-1850) erected in the year of his death after a fall from a favourite horse on Constitution Hill. The statue is by Matthew Noble (1818-76). Peel was noted for his administrative ability and intellectual honesty and Wellington remarked of him 'I never knew a man in whose truth and justice I had more lively confidence' but on another less harmonious occasion retorted 'I have no small talk and Peel has no manners'. Peel himself stated his philosophy quite plainly when he said 'As a minister of the Crown I reserve to myself, distinctly and unequivocally the right of adapting my conduct to the exigency of the moment' and this flexibility gave him rein to develop free trade, to introduce income tax on all incomes over £150 per annum and to change sides and support the Anti-Corn Law League after years spent opposing it. Peel is chiefly remembered now as founder of the modern police force, whose members were nicknamed 'Peelers' or 'Bobbies' — a name which still sticks today.

On the west side of the Square, the statue of **Abraham Lincoln** (1809-65), sixteenth President of the United States of America, is a copy of the fine statue by Augustus Saint-Gaudens at Chicago and was presented by the American people in 1920. Lincoln, bitterly opposed to slavery, was assassinated by John Wilkes Booth, a supporter of the southern states, while visiting Ford's Theatre, Washington, to see the play *Our American Cousin* at the end of the Civil War. As well as a lawyer and a statesman Lincoln had been a captain in the Black Hawk War of 1832 and told a good story against himself. One day part of his company was marching across a field and ahead was a gate through which Lincoln's troops would have to pass. He said later: 'I could not for the life of me remember the proper word of command for getting my company endwise. Finally, as we came near, I shouted: "This company is dismissed for two minutes when it will fall in again on the other side of the gate".' It is a comforting demonstration of the fallibility of even the most outstanding of men.

Also on the west side in the so-called 'Canning enclosure' is a bronze statue of **George Canning** (1770-1827) by Sir

Left: *The statue of George Canning, Pitt's protégé, stands in Parliament Square.*
Right: *The statue of President Lincoln in Parliament Square was presented by the American people in 1920.*

Richard Westmacott, erected in 1832. Canning was Foreign Secretary and after Lord Liverpool's death in 1827 George IV made him Prime Minister and Chancellor of the Exchequer. The cost of erecting the statue (£7,000) was borne by public subscription and after being placed in Palace Yard in 1832 it was moved to this site in 1867. Amidst all the stresses of office Canning kept his sense of humour, even to the extent of sending out ciphered messages in rhyme. On 31st January 1826, Sir Charles Bagot, English Ambassador to The Hague, must have been delighted to receive:

> In matters of commerce the fault of the Dutch
> Is offering too little and asking too much,
> The French are with equal advantage content

So we clap on Dutch bottoms just twenty per cent!

The superb statue of **Oliver Cromwell** (1599-1658) is by Sir William Hamo Thornycroft and stands outside Westminster Hall. It was erected in 1899 and shows Cromwell in uniform, bareheaded with his Bible and sword, thus succinctly reflecting two modern views of him. For was he the pious saviour of English freedom or just another ruthless dictator? Cromwell came to prominence in the Civil War of 1642-9, creating the New Model Army and becoming the greatest soldier in England, a remarkable achievement for a man with no military training. With needless brutality and butchery he crushed the resistance of the Irish Royalists ('not what they want but what is good for them') and this act was not easily forgotten. Even in 1895 Irish mem-

The striking upright posture of the statue of Richard I (Coeur-de-Lion) is complemented by the architecture of the Houses of Parliament which form its backdrop.

Oliver Cromwell with Bible and sword is outside Westminster Hall. Unfortunately his spurs are upside down.

Reliefs show the king in battle and the archer who fired the shot that mortally wounded him at the Castle of Chaluz being brought to the dying man for pardon. (In fact the archer was treacherously flayed alive the moment the king died.)

Across the road from Old Palace Yard is the national memorial to **George V** (1947) by Sir William Reid Dick (at one time President of the Royal Society of Sculptors and King's Sculptor in Ordinary) and Sir Giles Gilbert Scott. It was unveiled by George VI on 22nd October 1947 and is a full-length figure in the uniform of a field marshal with Garter robes and Sword of

George V, called 'the father of his people', adopted the family name of Windsor.

bers of Parliament strongly opposed the wish of the Liberal party to vote £500 towards the erection of this statue and in the end Lord Rosebery, Prime Minister at the time, decided to make a gift of it.

At the north end of Old Palace Yard is a magnificent bronze statue of **Richard I (Coeur-de-Lion)** (1157-99), probably England's most popular medieval king, by Baron Carlo Marochetti RA (1805-68), who came to England in the Piedmontese Revolution of 1848 and began a large practice which owed much of its success to royal patronage. This statue, considered to be the sculptor's *chef d'oeuvre*, in which the king holds his sword aloft, was put up in 1851 and well expresses Marochetti's famous flamboyance, which inflamed the critics, although his verve always fell short of vulgarity. The sword was bent by a bomb in the Second World War but has since been repaired.

The original of Rodin's sculpture 'The Burghers of Calais' is at Calais Town Hall; this copy stands in the Victoria Tower Gardens, Westminster.

State. The scheme for the provision of playing fields throughout the country is in association with the monument. Once at House of Commons Question Time, Mr Dudley Smith, MP for Warwick and Leamington, asked why this statue had carried a Campaign for Nuclear Disarmament symbol for over two years. Mr Mellish, the Minister of Public Building and Works, replied that all the statues and monuments under his care were normally inspected every three months. 'It certainly seems that we missed King George V', he said. 'I will look into this. I don't know why you saw the symbol and we didn't.' Mr Mellish then revealed that removing the symbol on 7th June 1968 took only fifteen minutes and cost 5 shillings.

In the Victoria Tower Gardens (which take their name from the Victoria Tower of the Houses of Parliament, on which, by day, the Union Jack flies to show that Parliament is in session) is a bronze group, **The Burghers of Calais** (1915) by Auguste Rodin, a replica of the statuary erected in Calais in 1895. The burghers agreed to surrender themselves to Edward III in 1340 with halters round their necks to save their town from destruction.

Mrs Emmeline Pankhurst (1858-1928), the leader of the movement for women's suffrage who was frequently arrested and imprisoned for her beliefs, has a statue with lorgnette by A. G. Walker, erected in 1930 and unveiled by Stanley Baldwin. Flowers are laid here each year by women who worked for the suffragette movement. Her daughter **Dame Christabel Pankhurst** (1881-1958), famous in the same field as her mother, is commemorated by a bronze medallion.

Further south in the Gardens is the Buxton Memorial Fountain by S. S. Teulon, 1865, which commemorates **Sir Thomas Fowell Buxton** (1786-1845), MP for Weymouth, who fought for the abolition of slavery in the British dominions and elsewhere and in 1824 became leader of the anti-slavery party. It was erected by his son Charles Buxton MP, in honour of his father's efforts to free colonial slaves. The eight decorative figures of British rulers, including Caractacus, Constantine, Canute, Alfred, William the Conqueror and Victoria, were stolen, four in 1960 and four in 1971, but were replaced by fibreglass figures in 1980.

To the west of Westminster Abbey by Broad Sanctuary is a red granite column by Scott with sculpture by J. B. Philip which commemorates the **Old Boys of Westminster School** who died in the Crimean War and Indian Mutiny.

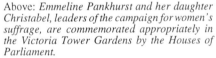

Above: *Emmeline Pankhurst and her daughter Christabel, leaders of the campaign for women's suffrage, are commemorated appropriately in the Victoria Tower Gardens by the Houses of Parliament.*

Left: *Many suffragettes suffered prison and humiliation before women's suffrage was achieved. Their monument is near New Scotland Yard.*

Further down Victoria Street by a lawn on the right- hand side is a plain and moving tall upright scroll which stands where Broadway skirts New Scotland Yard. On a stone column, the scroll of fibreglass finished in cold cast bronze, by Edwin Russell, was erected in 1970. The inscription reads: 'This tribute is erected by the **Suffragette** Fellowship to commemorate the courage and perseverance of all those men and women who in the long struggle for votes for women selflessly braved derision, opposition and ostracism, many enduring physical violence and suffering.'

Above left: *Marshal Foch's statue in Grosvenor Gardens was unveiled by the Prince of Wales, later Edward VIII.*

Above right: *Simón Bolívar, 'the Liberator', is immaculately tailored for Belgrave Square.*

Nineteenth-century maps show a surprisingly large area in Victoria marked 'Brewery'. This was the **Old Stag Brewery**, remembered today by Stag Place, opening from Bressenden Place, with a 20 foot metal stag in modernistic style by the sculptor Edward Bainbridge Copnall (1962).

At the south end of Grosvenor Gardens, facing Victoria station, is **Marshal Ferdinand Foch** (1851-1929) by G. Malissard, a copy of the statue at Cassel, France. It was given by France, unveiled by the Prince of Wales in June 1930 and commemorates France's most famous general and one of the outstanding Allied leaders of the First World War, who was made a field marshal of Britain and given the Order of Merit as an appreciation of his services.

A stylised aluminium stag recalls a former occupant of the site in Victoria — the Stag Brewery.

In the south-east corner of Belgrave Square is a statue by Hugo Daini (1974) of **Simón Bolívar** (1783-1830), who devoted his life to the cause of freeing the South American countries from Spanish domination. With British aid he succeeded and Venezuela, Ecuador, Colombia, Peru, Panama and Bolivia (named after Bolívar) were founded. The statue was erected in 1974 by the Council of Latin America and unveiled by James Callaghan, Foreign Secretary. Bolívar has been called 'the Washington of South America'. On the plinth are the words: 'I am convinced that England alone is capable of protecting the world's precious rights as she is great, glorious and wise.'

The Victorians liked to decorate bridges. When work on **Vauxhall Bridge** was completed in 1906 there was money to spare — a rare and fortunate circumstance. Large bronze statues, over twice life-sized, were erected to use up the available funds. Upstream, by F. W. Pomeroy, are Agriculture (scythe), Architecture (holding a model of St Paul's), Engineering and Pottery; downstream, by Alfred Drury, are Local Government, Science, Fine Arts (palette) and Education (books).

East of Vauxhall Bridge, by the river in Pimlico Gardens is a statue to **William Huskisson** (1770-1830), the statesman and the first man to be killed by a railway train. The statue is by John Gibson and shows Huskisson dressed as a Roman senator. It was described by Sir Osbert Sitwell as of 'Boredom rising from the bath'. The accident occurred at the opening of the Liverpool and Manchester Railway on 15th September 1830. The Duke of Wellington, Sir Robert Peel and Huskisson were amongst the large crowd of guests present and when the engines stopped to take in water at

Roman senatorial dress was a curious choice for William Huskisson, first victim of a railway accident. He stands in Pimlico Gardens.

Parkside Mr Huskisson strolled with the others along the line. As they returned to their seats a second train drew up: Huskisson tried to enter but the door swung back and he was thrown under the wheels. His thigh was crushed and mangled and he was heard to murmur: 'I have met my death.' This sad prophecy came true for he died that night in the parsonage at Eccles.

A statue of **Sir John Everett Millais** PRA (1829-96), brush and palette in hand, stands in the forecourt of the Tate Gallery, which he helped to found. Millais was a prodigy, the youngest ever pupil in the Royal Academy Schools in 1840, and in 1848, with Rossetti and Holman Hunt, a founder of the Pre-Raphaelite Brotherhood. Under the Brotherhood's influence he produced such famous works as 'The Carpenter's Shop' (1850) and in 1854 he married Ruskin's former wife Effie. His friendship with Ruskin foundered.

Millais then turned himself into a fashionable, technically brilliant, public artist, forsaking his Pre-Raphaelite theories. It is this image that the statue conveys. He painted costume history and *genre* pieces such as 'The Boyhood of Raleigh', 'The Order of Release' and 'Bubbles'. When a print of his 'Cherry Ripe' (for which his own children acted as models) was published as a supplement by *The Graphic* it sold 600,000 copies within a week. Towards august sitters for portraits, such as Gladstone, Disraeli and Carlyle, he showed a cheerful, confident face: when Cardinal Newman, attending for this purpose, hesitated momentarily to climb the model's 'throne', Millais encouraged him: 'Come, jump up, you dear old boy!' He was knighted in 1895, the first artist to be so honoured, and became President of the Royal Academy in 1896. He died during his year of office.

When Sir Henry Tate, the wealthy sugar refiner, financed the building of the Tate Gallery and gave his own collection of paintings to it, he required that there be a **Britannia** over the portico, flanked by a lion and a unicorn. The lion holds the royal arms (1897).

A **buttress from the Millbank Prison** (1816-90) was saved when the prison was demolished. It stood at the head of the river steps, down which, until 1867, some 1,100

Sir John Everett Millais first exhibited at the Royal Academy at the age of seventeen. He stands outside the Tate Gallery, Millbank.

prisoners sentenced to transportation to the colonies passed on their way to Australia. Millbank took its name from the smock mill on the river bank. In *David Copperfield* Charles Dickens gives a chilling description of the neighbourhood of the prison, which was in fact a model according with the ideals of the reformer Jeremy Bentham. The Tate Gallery stands on its site. In Atterbury Street, by the side of the Tate, is the Royal Army Medical Corps building with Matthew Noble's statue of **Sir James McGrigor** (1771-1854), former Director General.

» 4 «
CHELSEA AND WESTWARDS

In the Figure Court of Chelsea Hospital, an institution for old and invalid soldiers, built by Wren in 1682-92, is a statue in Roman dress of the founder, **Charles II** (1630-85), by Grinling Gibbons (1648-1721), a sculptor equally famous for his fine wood carving. This was yet another statue commissioned, like the James II in Trafalgar Square and the Charles II at Windsor, by Tobias Rustat, Yeoman of the Robes. On 29th May (Charles's birthday) the statue is wreathed in oak leaves to commemorate his hiding in the Boscobel oak on 6th September 1651 during his flight from the battle of Worcester. The Parliamentary troops searched the surrounding woods but the leaves hid the king and saved the monarchy. The pensioners, who wear a distinctive scarlet uniform on full-dress occasions, wear sprigs of oak leaves and receive double rations on Founder's Day.

In the hospital grounds is a granite **obelisk** (1853) by Cockerell to commemorate the victory of **Chillianwallah** on 13th January 1849 and it records the names of 250 men of the 24th Regiment killed during this notable battle of the Second Sikh War. After Sir Hugh Gough's decisive victory at Goojerat the Sikhs finally came under British rule.

In the Chelsea Physic Garden, established by the Apothecaries' Society in 1673, is a replica of a robed and wigged statue of **Sir Hans Sloane** (1737) by John Michael Rysbrack (1693-1770), one of a group of sculptors who dominated the early Georgian period. The original statue is in the foyer of the British Museum. Sloane, the physician and naturalist, presented the site of the garden to the society in 1722 on condition that 2,000 specimens of distinct plants grown there would be presented to the Royal Society (of which he was president from 1727 till 1740) 'well dried and preserved' in annual instalments of fifty — a condition that has been generously fulfilled. The annual rent is £5 and seeds and plants from the garden are still used for world-wide research. Here the first cedars grown in England were planted in 1683 and cotton seed was sent from here in 1732 to America to found the plantations of the south. Hans Crescent, Sloane Street and Sloane Square also perpetuate Sir Hans's memory.

The completion of Sir Joseph Bazalgette's work on the **Chelsea Embankment** in 1874 was marked by two columns with cherubs, one in the river wall, east of the Albert Bridge, the other at the end of Old Church Street.

In the gardens of the Embankment off Cheyne Row, to the west of Albert Bridge, is a statue of **Thomas Carlyle** (1795-1881), the essayist and historian (the 'Sage of Chelsea'), by Boehm. This statue, erected in 1882, is said to be an 'uncanny likeness' and shows Carlyle seated on his study chair with a pile of books beside him, looking thoughtfully across the Thames. In 1929 a copy was given to his birthplace of Ecclefechan by his nephew and was unveiled by the donor's grand-daughter. The Carlyles

On 29th May, his birthday, Charles II's statue at Chelsea Hospital is decked with oak leaves.

moved to London in 1834 and lived at 24 Cheyne Walk (now a National Trust property with Carlyle relics), where in 1837 he wrote *The French Revolution*, the work which was to bring him fame and membership of a literary circle which included John Stuart Mill and Leigh Hunt. As an historian Carlyle had his critics, who accused him, with some justification, of an obsession with violence and a contempt for the rights of ordinary individuals, but his vibrant, rhetorical prose, which broke so completely with the dry style of earlier historians, caused another critic to remark: 'As a picturesque historian Carlyle has no equal.' As Carlyle himself said: 'Macaulay is well for a while, but one wouldn't *live* under Niagara.'

Near the Carlyle monument in the same gardens is a memorial bird-bath by Charles James Pibworth to **Margaret Damer Dawson OBE** (1875-1920), who lived at 10 Cheyne Walk. Miss Dawson, a gifted musician and an enthusiastic advocate of animal protection, founded the Women's Police Service in 1915 and became its Chief Officer.

A bronze nude entitled 'Atalanta' by **Francis Derwent Wood** was erected by the end of Albert Bridge in 1929 as a tribute to the artist, who died in 1926, from his friends, especially those in the Chelsea Arts Club.

St Thomas More's statue stands outside Chelsea Old Church, where he once worshipped with a humility that prompted him to sing in the choir dressed in an ordinary surplice. 'God's body, my Lord Chancellor, a parish clerk?' said the Duke of Norfolk when he saw him. Thomas More (1478-1535), brilliant, witty, civilised, a Renaissance scholar, author of *Utopia* (1516), a dream of an ideal state, was one of a group embracing Erasmus and John Colet. He succeeded Wolsey as Lord Chancellor 1529-

Left: *In Chelsea one can see the signature of the sculptor, L. Cubitt Bevis, on St Thomas More's large hat.*

Right: *Thomas Carlyle, 'the Sage of Chelsea', whose Cheyne Walk home belongs to the National Trust, is seated at Chelsea Embankment gardens.*

32 and while his relationship with Henry VIII had formerly been jovial and intimate he (like Becket) proved to be an obdurate chancellor. He disagreed strongly with the king's wish to divorce Catherine of Aragon, to relax the heresy laws and enhance royal supremacy. In 1532 he resigned, incurring Henry's fury for refusing to sign the compulsory oath conceding these points. He was imprisoned in the Tower of London, tried, found guilty of treason and executed on 6th July 1535. Following the practice of the time, he was buried in the Tower chapel of St Peter ad Vincula and his head, as befitted a 'traitor', nailed up on London Bridge. But it has long been a tradition that his daughter Margaret Roper secretly retrieved the body and had it moved to Chelsea.

He was canonised by the Catholic church in 1935.

Erasmus and Holbein were visitors when More and his family settled in Chelsea, in Beaufort House with its garden running down to the river. L. Cubitt Bevis's gilded and glowing statue shows More seated, in Chancellor's robes with his chain of office with Tudor rose emblem across his knees. The statue was unveiled by Dr Henry King, Speaker of the House of Commons, on 21st July 1969 and was — appropriately, for More was and still is very much a man of Chelsea — made possible by an appeal organised by local people. It was an imaginative touch to include More's facsimile signature on the plinth with the words 'Scholar, Saint, Statesman'.

Much further west, at Barnes, is a memorial to More's friend **John Colet** (1467?-1519), the great reforming Dean of St Paul's and principal Christian humanist of his day, founder of St Paul's School. The statue, by William Hamo Thornycroft (1902), regarded by many as the sculptor's finest work, shows the robed Colet seated, supported by two kneeling scholars with books. Colet, a lifelong friend of Erasmus and son of a Lord Mayor of London, was the only survivor of 22 children. He thus inherited a fortune, which he devoted to refounding St Paul's School. The school moved from St Paul's Churchyard to Hammersmith Road in 1884 and to Barnes in 1968, taking the statue with it. In 1944 the buildings became the headquarters of Field Marshal Montgomery (himself an Old Pauline) during the planning of the Normandy invasion. Discipline, austerity and plain speaking marked Colet's character. It seems that the two men had something in common.

A rather out of the way memorial is at the Mile Post on the Surrey Bank, Putney-Mortlake footpath, SW14, on the stretch of the Thames used for the Oxford and Cambridge Boat Race. It commemorates **Stephen Fairbairn** (1862-1938), a non-practising barrister who rowed for four years for Cambridge University and also for his college, Jesus. But he is chiefly remembered for his brilliant, innovative coaching in the 'Fairbairn style', and his work to increase the understanding and popularity of the sport of rowing. An 11 foot obelisk was put up in 1963 on the spot where he would stand to watch the rowing. It was unveiled by Viscount Bruce of Melbourne, former Prime Minister of Australia, and it includes a bronze medallion of Fairbairn by G. C. Drinkwater.

In The Mall stands Captain Cook, in unseamanlike pose with his foot on a coil of rope.

» 5 «
THE MALL, PALL MALL, ST JAMES'S, ST JAMES'S PARK

From Trafalgar Square, The Mall leads to Buckingham Palace. **Admiralty Arch**, an extension of the Admiralty, whose triple arches can be closed by massive iron gates, has a fine view of The Mall, with Buckingham Palace at the west end. It was designed by Sir Aston Webb in 1910 as part of the national memorial to Queen Victoria.

On the left beyond the arch is a statue of **Captain James Cook** (1728-79), put up in 1914, in a dangerous and uncharacteristic pose for an expert seaman, with his foot resting on a coil of rope. Cook, explorer and circumnavigator, is by Sir Thomas Brock RA (1847-1922), a leading Victorian sculptor whose work showed dignity and refinement. Cook is especially connected with explorations in Australasia and his travels are remembered in the names Cook Strait and Cook Islands. He himself named the Society Islands in honour of the Royal Society. His fatal last voyage, on which he discovered the Sandwich or Hawaiian Islands, where he was eventually killed by the natives in 1779, began on 25th June 1776.

In The Mall, immediately opposite the Cook statue is the **Royal Marines Memorial** to those who fell in China and in the Boer War in South Africa. It is by Adrian Jones and was erected in 1903. The battle scenes are by Sir Thomas Graham Jackson; one shows the Chinese attack on the Peking legation, the other the action at Graspan in South Africa. A defiant marine with bayonet and rifle protects a fallen comrade.

At the junction of Cockspur Street and Pall Mall East is a statue (1836) of **George III**, the first of the Hanoverians to firmly identify himself with Britain. In the speech from the throne in 1760 he said: 'Born and educated in this country I glory in the name of Briton.' The sculptor was Matthew Cotes Wyatt (1777-1862), the son of James Wyatt, the noted architect. Early in life Wyatt was employed at Windsor Castle and became a favourite of the king and queen, a fact which brought many commissions his way — although he described himself as an amateur, a title belied by the size of his *oeuvre*. In 1832 a committee of subscribers commissioned this statue to commemorate the late king and it is regarded as Wyatt's best work, with vitality and verisimilitude.

At the foot of Lower Regent Street is the **Guards Monument** of 1859, which commemorates the 22,162 guardsmen who fell in the Crimean War. The monument, by John Bell, who was often employed on official commissions, has figures of guardsmen cast from captured Russian guns and the guns piled at the back were actually used at the siege of Sebastopol.

To the right is a statue (1862) by John Foley (1818-74) of **Sidney Herbert, 1st Baron Herbert of Lea** (1810-61), Secretary for War during the Crimean War, and

Above: *The Isle of Portland provided stone for many London monuments. This one at the southern end of Lower Regent Street commemorates the Crimean dead and is flanked by Florence Nightingale and her supporter Sidney Herbert.*

Below: *This plaque on the plinth of Florence Nightingale's statue shows wounded soldiers arriving at Scutari Hospital in the Crimean War.*

to the left is his friend **Florence Nightingale** (1820-1910), renowned for her work in the hospital at Scutari. Her statue, by Arthur George Walker (born 1861), whose work was exhibited from 1884 to the middle of the twentieth century, has bronze reliefs showing Miss Nightingale in the Crimea, interviewing officers, attending a meeting of nurses and arranging the transport of the wounded. A crisp story is told of John Bright, who when passing the statue was asked by his son the meaning of the word 'Crimea', to which Bright replied 'A crime'.

Edward VII and Queen Alexandra lived at Marlborough House until he succeeded to the throne. Her memorial is in the garden wall; water flows behind the grating.

Above: *Pallas Athene's gilded statue is over the entrance to the Athenaeum Club in Waterloo Place.*

The stately Athenaeum Club, the leading club for academics, with many bishops among its members, stands at the south-west corner of Waterloo Place. It was founded in 1824 for 'scientific and literary men and artists'. Over the entrance stands a gilded figure of **Pallas Athene** by E. H. Baily (also responsible for Nelson, nearby). She was to be the only decoration for a building designed by Decimus Burton but a founder member and MP named Croker particularly wanted a frieze and, using some £2,000 subscribed by members for the provision of an icehouse, a frieze was ordered from John Henning with figures from those of the Parthenon. The wags were ready:

I'm John Wilson Croker,
I do as I please,
You asked for an icehouse,
I gave you a frieze!

The national memorial to **Edward VII**, a fleshy equestrian bronze (1921) by Sir Bertram Mackennal, the Australian sculptor who also designed the coinage on the accession of George V, stands in the centre of the southern part of Waterloo Place. To the east is a statue of **Captain Robert Falcon Scott** (1868-1912), the Antarctic explorer, which was given by the officers of the fleet in 1915 and which also commemorates his companions on his final journey to the South Pole, Oates, Bowers, Wilson and Evans. The statue, made by Lady Scott, shows the explorer dressed for the Antarctic with a ski-stick in his hand. Scott organised a series of expeditions and in 1910 sailed in the *Terra Nova* in an attempt to be the first to reach the South Pole. His party was just beaten by the Norwegian Amundsen and, disheartened by failure and dogged by bad

Below: *The national memorial to Edward VII in Waterloo Place is by the Australian Sir Bertram Mackennal.*

luck and appalling weather, they died on the homeward journey. Their papers were recovered and published in 1913 as *Scott's Last Expedition* together with his moving *Message to the Public*: 'Had we lived I should have had a tale to tell of the hardihood, endurance and courage of my companions which would have stirred the heart of every Englishman. These rough notes and our dead bodies must tell the tale.' His wife received the title of Lady Scott, an honour she would have received had he returned. Their son, Peter Markham Scott, was the world-famous painter, writer and naturalist, founder of the Wildfowl and Wetland Trust at Slimbridge.

Next to Scott is **Sir Colin Campbell, Baron Clyde** (1792-1863), the son of a Glasgow carpenter, who rose to high rank in the Army and fought at Chillianwallah in the Second Sikh War. Later he commanded the Highland Brigade in the Crimea and, when appointed Commander-in-Chief by Palmerston, succeeded in stamping out the Indian Mutiny in a few months.

At the corner is **John Laird Mair, 1st Baron Lawrence** (1811-79), by Sir Joseph Edgar Boehm, 1882. Lawrence entered the Indian Civil Service in 1829 and worked in the Delhi area: when the news of the Mutiny reached him he raised an army of 59,000 men and after a three-month siege captured the city of Delhi. He was hailed 'Saviour of India' and created a baronet on his return to England, with a pension of £2,000 a year. In 1863 he became Governor-General of India. The statue's inscription, 'How youngly he began to serve his country, how long continued', comes from *Coriolanus*.

Across the car park, near the Athenaeum is **Sir John Franklin** (1786-1847), the Arctic explorer, who died trying to find the North-west Passage to the Pacific. The

Above: *Robert Falcon Scott's statue in Waterloo Place was the work of his wife.*

Below: *Lawrence, 'Saviour of India', is commemorated in Waterloo Place.*

Queen Anne, outside 13 Queen Anne's Gate since 1708 at least, is one of London's most charming statues.

Peter Pan, probably the best loved statue in London, was erected in Kensington Gardens by private arrangement between Barrie and the Commissioner of Works.

Franklin discovered the North-west Passage but died doing so. This plaque on his statue in Waterloo Place shows his funeral on board ship.

statue, by Matthew Noble, was erected in 1866.

Also on this side is **Sir John Fox Burgoyne** (1782-1871), the natural son of General John Burgoyne and the opera singer Susan Caulfield. He joined Wellington in Portugal in 1809, fought with success at the sieges of Badajoz and Ciudad Rodrigo and later in the Crimea and became a field marshal in 1869. His statue is by Boehm, 1877.

Number 1 Carlton House Terrace was the home of **George Nathaniel, 1st Marquess Curzon of Kedleston** (1859-1925), and his statue by Sir Bertram Mackennal faces his former home at the corner of Carlton Gardens. Curzon, Viceroy of India, was often criticised for his rigid and autocratic ways although his fine oratory was admired. In 1919 he became Foreign Secretary, a post which he held with great success, and in 1923 he hoped to become Prime Minister in succession to Bonar Law but the honour went to Stanley Baldwin and Curzon never recovered from his bitter personal disappointment.

The cross of Lorraine and General Charles de Gaulle's inspiring words of 8th June 1940 — 'France has lost a battle but has not lost the War' — appear on the memorial on the wartime headquarters of the **Free**

French forces at 4 Carlton Gardens.

There are probably more statues of **Queen Victoria** (1819-1901) than of any other personage in the history of the human race. A regal-looking marble statue by Sir Thomas Brock (1897), under the porchway of the National Portrait Gallery annexe at 15 Carlton House Terrace, is one of them. It used to be in the Constitutional Club.

Victoria, who succeeded to the British throne in 1837 at the age of eighteen and reigned for 63 years, was married to her cousin Albert of Saxe-Coburg-Gotha (1819-61) for 21 years and bore him four sons and five daughters. She was related, either directly or by marriage, to most of the royal houses of Europe. The industrial revolution, the rise of the middle classes,

A stout Queen Victoria, once in the Constitutional Club and now on Carlton House Terrace, suffers from a chipped nose.

Waterloo Place, Carlton House Terrace

social reform, scientific and medical advance, the apogee of empire, a distinctive artistic style and a sense of union and security never again experienced are all hallmarks of the period known as 'Victorian'. Victoria was a personality even at the age of eighteen. Of her first Privy Council meeting only some two hours after she succeeded to the throne, the Duke of Wellington commented: 'Five feet high, but she not only filled her chair but the room.'

At the south end of Waterloo Place rises one of London's most spectacular monuments, the Duke of York's Column, erected in 1833 with a bronze statue by Sir Richard Westmacott of **Frederick Augustus, Duke of York and Albany**, who died in 1827. Westmacott was a lifelong exponent of the classical in sculpture, a style he learned in his early years in Rome and Florence. This pink granite monument, a tall finger against the trees of the park, is to the second son of George III, a rather mediocre soldier, who was immortalised in the rhyme, current for over a century, but first printed in Arthur Rackham's *Mother Goose* in 1913:

O, the Grand Old Duke of York,
He had ten thousand men,
He marched them up to the top of the hill,
And he marched them down again,
And when they were up, they were up,
And when they were down, they were down,
And when they were only halfway up,
They were neither up nor down!

The Duke, 13 feet high, weighs 7 tons and is of Aberdeen granite. An interior stairway of 169 steps leads to the top of the column (no access) and the monument cost £30,000. The Duke was popularly said to have taken refuge from his creditors on top of his column and wags remarked that the light-

George VI, in the uniform of Admiral of the Fleet, overlooks The Mall by Carlton House Terrace.

ning conductor on his head would make a convenient spike for his bills! The monument, which bears no inscription, was paid for by stopping one day's pay from every officer and man in the British Army, which made him an extremely unpopular ex-Commander-in-Chief, a post he held from 1798. He lost the position in 1809 following scandals connected with his mistress, Mary Anne Clarke, but was reinstated in 1811 and one of his more useful activities was to found the Duke of York's Royal Military School.

Steps leading down from Carlton House Terrace pass the statue of **George VI** (1895-1952) by William Macmillan, in the Garter mantle over the undress uniform of an Admiral of the Fleet. The architectural setting was designed by Louis de Soissons and the statue was unveiled in 1955.

To the north, across Pall Mall, in St James's Square is a very late rococo equestrian statue of **William III** (1650-1702) by J. Bacon the Younger (1800), a beautiful work too little appreciated. In 1724 Samuel Travers left 'sufficient money to purchase and erect in St James's Square, an equestrian statue in brass to the glorious memory of my master King William the Third'. The stone was duly put up but no statue was forthcoming and nothing further was done about the bequest till a record of the will was found in 1806 and steps taken to comply with Travers's wishes. William met his death at Hampton Court when his horse tripped and fell over a molehill (which is realistically shown under the horse's feet). Jacobite adherents subsequently toasted the mole — 'The little gentleman in the velvet jacket'.

Against the railings at the north-east corner of the square is the memorial to **Woman Police Constable Yvonne Fletcher**, killed during the siege of the Libyan Embassy in April 1984.

Returning to The Mall, between St James's Palace and Marlborough House, one passes, in the wall of Marlborough House, an *art nouveau* memorial (1926) to **Queen Alexandra** (1844-1925), consort of Edward VII, who lived and died there. The memorial fountain is by Sir Alfred Gilbert, born in 1854 and a student of Boehm, who became an RA in 1892 and whose other works include the Eros in Piccadilly.

Also in the garden wall, but facing The Mall, is a bronze medallion of **Queen Mary** (1867-1953), consort to George V. It was erected in 1967 and is by Sir William Reid Dick. Queen Mary was noted for her un-

At Duke of York Steps by The Mall the 'Grand Old Duke of York' on his column surveys the War Office. Richard Westmacott, the sculptor, received a fee of £7,000 for the statue.

_*The Mall*   *49*

Above: *The national memorial to Queen Victoria, in front of Buckingham Palace, makes an impressive traffic island.*

Above: *This medallion portrait, in the wall of her former home, Marlborough House, confirms Queen Mary's loyalty to Edwardian styles.*

(1819-1901) which is 13 feet high and on the other sides are groups representing Motherhood, Justice, Peace and Progress, Science and Art, Industry and Agriculture and Naval and Military Power. The whole composition is 82 feet high and 2,300 tons of marble were used in its making. Its creator, Sir Thomas Brock, was made

Below: *Policewoman Yvonne Fletcher was killed during the Libyan Embassy siege in 1984.*

changing fashions, her characteristic 'toque' hats and her collection of antiques.

At the west end of The Mall, in front of Buckingham Palace, is the **Queen Victoria Memorial** (of which the design of The Mall itself forms a part). This memorial, the perfect distillation of later Victorian taste, was set up in 1911 and is mainly of white marble. It was designed by Sir Aston Webb with sculptures by Sir Thomas Brock and the central pedestal is crowned by a gilded and winged Victory with Courage and Constancy at her feet. At the base on the east side is a seated figure of Queen Victoria

Knight Commander of the Bath on the platform during the unveiling ceremony. Note that the queen wears her wedding ring on her right hand as she did in life — to please Albert's German tastes.

It was announced in February 1992 that approval had been granted for a memorial to the 1,600,000 **Canadians who served with British forces** in two world wars to be erected near Canada Gates in Green Park near Buckingham Palace. The idea was first mooted in 1988 in a letter to *The Daily Telegraph.*

Across St James's Park, a statue of **Field Marshal Earl Alexander of Tunis** is appropriately sited in front of the Guards'

Following his army career Alexander became a popular Governor-General of Canada.

Headquarters, Birdcage Walk. He was colonel of the Irish Guards 1946-9. The bronze statue by James Butler was unveiled by Queen Elizabeth II on 9th May 1985 to mark the completion of a 22-year-long project to rebuild the London headquarters of the Brigade of Guards. It shows Alexander in campaign kit of sheepskin jacket, high boots and binoculars.

Alexander (1891-1969) was an outstanding military figure of the Second World War. In a last-minute appointment in 1940 he led the rearguard action at Dunkirk, helping to save more British troops than anyone believed possible. In 1942 he commanded the retreat from Burma, again intent on saving life. He was Commander-in-Chief in North Africa in 1942, giving Montgomery freedom to carry through his own plans for El Alamein and fully supporting him with troops and supplies. In 1943-5 he was overall commander in the Sicilian and Italian campaigns. After the war he spent a period as an exceptionally popular Governor-General of Canada and a less happy one as Minister of Defence in Churchill's government 1952-4. He resigned in 1954.

Between the Guards' Headquarters and Horse Guards Road, an alleyway leads to Queen Anne's Gate, one of London's handsomest streets. Here is an attractive weathered statue of **Queen Anne** (1665-1714) which has stood outside Number 13 at least since 1708. It was made for the portico of St Mary-le-Strand, one of the earliest of the fifty churches designed by order of Queen Anne, always, as her friend Sarah, Duchess of Marlborough, remarked, 'religious without affectation', but it was never erected there. There is a possibility that it is the work of Francis Bird, who also made the earlier Queen Anne which once stood outside St Paul's.

» 6 «
PICCADILLY

In the centre of Piccadilly Circus is the Shaftesbury Memorial, 1893, by Sir Alfred Gilbert, a fountain surmounted by a winged figure of an archer universally known as Eros although the sculptor intended it to represent the Angel of Christian Charity (with perhaps a neat, built-in pun on Shaftesbury's name for the archer is 'burying a shaft'). It was the first statue to be made of aluminium and so light that the sculptor could carry it across his studio. It commemorates the **7th Earl of Shaftesbury** (1801-85), the reformer and philanthropist who worked for a change in the lunacy laws and for factory improvements and promoted 'ragged schools' and the welfare of children. Warm-hearted Shaftesbury exclaimed, when, at the age of 84, he realised that the end of his life was approaching: 'I cannot bear to leave the world with all the misery in it.'

On the south side of Piccadilly is St James's Church, built by Sir Christopher Wren in 1684 and his only West End church. It was rebuilt after bombing in the Second World War and a **memorial garden** in front is dedicated to the 'courage and fortitude of the people of London'. At the west end is a memorial fountain by A. Hardiman

to **Julian Salter Elias, Viscount Southwood**, the philanthropist and newspaper owner (1873-1946) who paid for the laying out of the garden.

At Burlington House, on the north side of the street, the home of the Royal Academy of Arts, is a statue in the quadrangle to **Sir Joshua Reynolds** (1723-92) with brush and palette in hand. The statue is considered to be one of the best works of Alfred Drury (1856-1944), a sculptor whose active work continued into the reign of Edward VII. Reynolds was one of the original members of the Academy, founded in 1768, and its first president. He was a portrait painter who founded the Royal Academy Schools and whose writings are still of the greatest value to students of painting, and the English successor to Van Dyck. He was a Devon man who came to London in 1753 and stayed for life. His kindly good sense was legendary; in a discourse to the Royal Academy's students in 1769 he said, 'If you have great talents, industry will prove them; if you have moderate abilities, industry will supply their deficiency' — wise words for anyone at the outset of a career.

Left: *'Eros' in Piccadilly Circus is probably the most photographed memorial in the world.*

Left: *Sir Joshua Reynolds stands in the quadrangle of Burlington House, home of the Royal Academy of Arts, of which he was the first president.*

Right: *London's public buildings are rich in façade decorations. One of those at the Museum of Mankind is Adam Smith, political economist and author of 'The Wealth of Nations'.*

Hundreds of small statues decorate the façades of London buildings. There are, for example, 370 on the outside of the Houses of Parliament alone and many more on such government buildings as the Foreign Office, the Victoria and Albert Museum and the Public Record Office. **The Museum of Mankind** on the south side of Burlington Gardens has 22 statues of great philosophers, writers and scientists in niches on its façade, including those of Newton, Bentham, Milton, Harvey, Galileo, Goethe, Leibnitz, Linnaeus, Hunter, Hume, Davy, Adam Smith, Locke and Bacon. The building, by Sir James Pennethorne, was constructed in 1866-9 as headquarters for the University of London. It now houses the Ethnography Department of the British Museum, renamed in 1972 the Museum of Mankind.

» 7 «

HYDE PARK CORNER, HYDE PARK

Opposite Apsley House, which stands at the west end of Piccadilly and was once known as Number 1 London since it was the first house inside the Hyde Park turnpike gate, is a bronze statue of **Arthur Wellesley, 1st Duke of Wellington** (1769-1852). It shows the Duke riding Copenhagen, the horse which carried him for over sixteen hours at the battle of Waterloo and which was honourably retired to the Duke's country home, Stratfield Saye, and eventually buried with full military honours; the horse's tombstone bears the words: 'God's humbler instrument, though meaner clay, Shall share the glory of that glorious day.' Forty horses were needed to drag the stone figure of Copenhagen to the site. The Duke is guarded by a Grenadier, a Royal Highlander, a Welch Fusilier and an Inniskilling Dragoon and the statue faces his old home, now the Wellington Museum, where on the anniversary of the battle Wellington's officers would dine with their commander-in-chief in the Waterloo Chamber. The figures are cast from twelve French cannon captured in Wellington's battles. The 'Iron Duke', usually remembered exclusively for his military activities and greatly admired by his troops (one infantry captain said 'We would rather see his long nose in a fight than a reinforcement of ten thousand any day'), had a gentler side to his character. A pleasant story is told of an occasion when he found a small boy crying because he was going away to school next day and was worried about the welfare of his pet toad in his absence. The Duke took full particulars, promising to look into the matter, and in due course the boy received a letter at school: 'Field Marshal the Duke of Wellington presents his compliments to Master — and has the pleasure to inform him that his toad is well.'

The figure of *David* (1925) leaning on Goliath's sword is by Francis Derwent Wood RA, who exhibited from 1895 at the Slade, South Kensington and Royal Academy Art Schools: he later entered the studio of Brock and became Professor of Sculpture at South Kensington. This figure forms the **Machine Gun Corps Memorial** with the unusually frank inscription: 'Saul hath slain his thousands but David his tens of thousands.'

Also on this traffic island is the Wellington Arch built by Decimus Burton and which originally stood opposite the main entrance to Hyde Park and was moved here in 1883 when the crowning statue of Wellington was taken down and sent to Aldershot.

The group which surmounts it is of Peace in her quadriga and dates from 1912. It was given by Lord Michelham in memory of **Edward VII**. Captain Adrian Jones, its sculptor, spent 23 years in the cavalry (which included three campaigns), then turned successfully to sculpture. This work, which took four years to complete, is regarded as his crowning achievement. His skill at depicting horses was, not surprisingly, legendary and this piece has the unusual quality of presenting an almost identical silhou-

Above: *In 1887 Wellington's equestrian statue by Wyatt was moved from the arch at Hyde Park Corner and taken to Aldershot. It was replaced by the smaller one by Boehm on the opposite page.*

Below: *Peace in her quadriga, on the Wellington Arch. The model for the quadriga's driver was the eleven-year-old son of the donor, Lord Michelham.*

ette from either side. Before the quadriga was set up Captain Jones entertained a group of friends to tea inside the horses.

Close by is one of the most moving monuments in London, the **Royal Artillery War Memorial** by Charles Sargeant Jagger and Lionel Pearson, a massive construction very suitable for its site, which takes the form of a huge gun with bronze figures on four sides and a macabre inscription: 'Here was a royal fellowship of death.' The gun is a howitzer, used in siege work, and is so positioned that a shell from it would, given sufficient charge, land on the Somme battlefield in France, where the Royal Artillery lost so many men in the First World War. The howitzer is an odd choice of gun, for the Royal Artillery was best known for its field guns.

In Hyde Park itself, on the left of the ring

At Hyde Park Corner the Duke of Wellington by Boehm rides Copenhagen, who carried him for sixteen hours at Waterloo.

A shell from the 9.2 inch howitzer on the Royal Artillery War Memorial, with adequate charge, would land on the Somme battlefield.

The 33 ton Achilles in Hyde Park has been called the 'most impressive statue in London' but it is neither Achilles nor Wellington, whom it commemorates.

road from Hyde Park Corner to Marble Arch, is a colossal bronze figure known as the **Achilles Statue** (the 'Ladies' Trophy') by Sir Richard Westmacott RA. This figure, erected in 1822, is really a copy of one of the horse-tamers on the Monte Catallo in Rome and not Achilles at all. It cost £10,000 and was paid for by the women of England to commemorate the Duke of Wellington. The naive subscribers were rudely surprised by the statue's nakedness when it finally appeared! It was cast from cannon captured in the Peninsular War and although it was not intended as a likeness visitors expected the face to be Wellington's. One Napoleonic veteran visiting London in 1850, and depressed by the great quantity of Wellingtoniana everywhere, exclaimed with relief when he looked at it: 'Enfin, on est vengé!'

To the right on another traffic island is a statue of **Lord Byron** (1880) by Richard C. Belt, a great portraitist of the Victorian period, which shows Byron meditating on a rock accompanied by his favourite dog, 'Boatswain'. This was one of the sculptor's failures. Byron would have understood, for he wrote:

To have, when the original is dust,
A name, a wretched picture and a worse
   bust ...

The marble for the statue (*rosso antico*), in a block weighing 57 tons, was given by the people of Greece. A friend remarked that the statue 'does not in the remotest degree resemble Byron either in face or figure'.

To the north of the Serpentine (an artificial lake of about 40 acres in Hyde Park) is a bird sanctuary adorned by the figure of

Rima by Jacob Epstein (1880-1959), one of sculpture's greatest figures and by far the most controversial of the twentieth century. Rima, a memorial to **William Henry Hudson** (1841-1922), the author and naturalist, is the Spirit of Nature in Hudson's book *Green Mansions* and Epstein's immense and sometimes gross symbolism aroused such feeling that on at least two occasions the statue has been tarred and feathered!

A granite rock, nearly 7 feet high, placed on three smaller stones, stands behind the Serpentine boathouse. The inscription reads: 'This boulder was brought here from Norway, where it was worn and shaped for thousands of years by forces of nature — frost, running water, rock, sand and ice, until it obtained its present shape'; and on the front, 'This stone was erected by the **Royal Norwegian Navy and the Norwegian Merchant Fleet** in the year 1978. We thank the British people for friendship and hospitality during the Second World War. You gave us a safe haven in our common struggle for freedom and peace.' When Norway was forced to surrender to the Ger-

'Mad, bad and dangerous to know' was Lady Caroline Lamb's verdict on Lord Byron, whose statue in Hyde Park hardly bears out these vivid epithets.

mans in 1940, a large proportion of her vast fleet of merchant ships — greatly to Britain's benefit — sailed for British ports and with the Royal Norwegian Navy continued the battle from Britain.

The figure of Rima — Epstein's W. H. Hudson memorial — has twice been tarred and feathered.

The Albert Memorial facing the Royal Albert Hall is one of London's greatest landmarks.

Figures depicted in relief around the base of the Albert Memorial include a group of composers: Mozart, Mendelssohn, Weber, Haydn, Beethoven, Tallis, Gibbons, Lawes and Purcell.

» 8 «
KNIGHTSBRIDGE AND KENSINGTON

In Hans Crescent, by the side of Harrods, is a memorial to **Stephen Dodd, Noel Lane and Jane Arbuthnot** of the police force, killed by an IRA bomb in December 1983. The marble stone stands against the wall between two windows of the famous store.

Cardinal John Henry Newman (1801-90) will always be associated with the Brompton Oratory, Brompton Road, and in its grounds is his statue by Chavalliaud, in high Italian taste, which would have pleased Newman, who was converted to Roman Catholicism in 1845 and later introduced the Institute of the Oratory to England. He was the founder of the Oxford Movement and writer of the favourite hymn *Lead, kindly light.*

At the corner of Exhibition Road and Kensington Road stand the buildings of the Royal Geographical Society and high on the walls are statues of **Sir Ernest Shackleton** (1874-1922), who was presented with the Society's special gold medal after his party had in 1908 reached the farthest point south attained in Antarctica, and of **David Livingstone**, the African explorer (1813-73). In the forecourt is a bust of **Sir Clements Markham** (1830-1916), the geographer and life-long friend and historian of the Peruvian people, whose government erected this memorial. In 1860 he led an expedition to collect cinchona trees and seeds in the Eastern Andes and arranged their acclimatisation in India. This was a great success and resulted in a supply of quinine at a very low price.

Facing the Albert Hall is the celebrated **Albert Memorial**, the national monument to Prince Albert of Saxe-Coburg-Gotha, consort of Victoria, by Sir G. Gilbert Scott, 1872. The statue, unveiled by Victoria, cost £50,000. It shows the prince reading the catalogue of the Great Exhibition of 1851 and is by John Foley RA (1818-74). Foley, perhaps since Chantrey the finest British sculptor, came to England from Ireland in 1834 and later showed 49 works at the Royal Academy. This statue, commissioned by Victoria, is regarded as his finest work.

The memorial has allegorical figures in the Victorian manner representing Agriculture, Manufacture, Commerce and Engineering, Africa, America, Asia and Europe and reliefs of artists, men of letters, musicians, sculptors and painters. The whole monument, reminiscent of an Eleanor cross, cost £120,000 and is probably the most complete expression of Victorian taste to be seen in England today. Among the sculptors associated with it were John Bell, Patrick Macdonell, Thomas Thornycroft, John Lawlor, William Theed Jnr, Henry Weekes and Henry Hugh Armstead.

Behind the Albert Hall is a bronze statue of **Prince Albert** designed in 1858 by Joseph Durham (1822-77), whose practice was immense and well-merited. His purity of outline and accuracy rank him near Chantrey. This statue is a memorial to the Great Exhibition of 1851, of which the prince was the creator, and it overlooks the group of science and art institutions of the

Cardinal Newman, outside the Brompton Oratory, is holding his cardinal's hat.

and had leapt to fame in the defence of Mafeking when he and his troops were besieged for 217 days by the Boers. Baden-Powell was mentioned in dispatches and became a national hero. In 1908, at the age of 51, using some of the lessons of camping and woodcraft learned in campaigning days, he formed the Boy Scouts. He explained his object in these words in *Scouting for Boys*: 'The Scouts' motto is founded on my initials. It is : BE PREPARED, which means, you are always to be in a state of readiness in mind and body to do your duty.' Two years later he retired from the Army to give his full attention to the growing movement, which attracted over 100,000 members in two years. For girls the parallel Girl Guides movement was started.

In a niche on the Royal Geographic Society building is Sir Ernest Shackleton, the polar explorer.

sort dear to his heart.

Queen's Gate has an equestrian statue of **Robert Cornelis, 1st Baron Napier of Magdala** (1810-90), who received his title in 1868. He is chiefly remembered for his capture of the fortress of Magdala in Abyssinia after a gruelling 400 mile march which lasted ten weeks. The statue is by Sir Joseph Edgar Boehm.

Few really successful organisations escape their share of jokes and denigration and the Boy Scouts are no exception. Yet what other international youth movement can claim to have inspired every rising generation for nearly 85 years? The movement was founded by **Lieutenant-General Robert Stephenson Smyth Baden-Powell**. He had enjoyed an adventurous army career

Cornish granite was the intractable material chosen by Donald Potter for Baden-Powell's statue at Queen's Gate.

Baden-Powell, who was raised to the peerage in 1929, taking as his title Baron Baden-Powell of Gilwell (Gilwell, Essex, was an early training centre for scoutmasters), was a versatile man who wrote widely on military history, his own reminiscences, scouting and sport, exhibited sculpture at the Royal Academy in 1907 and sketched. His Cornish granite statue by Donald Potter (who had himself benefited from the Scout movement) stands at the corner of Queen's Gate and was unveiled in 1961 by the Duke of Gloucester, president of the Boy Scouts' Association. It shows Baden-Powell in Scout uniform, bareheaded and wearing, as he liked to do, a cavalry cloak. The famous Boy Scout hat is in his hand.

At the north end of Long Water (the part of the Serpentine in Kensington Gardens) is a statue by Calder Marshall (1858) of **Edward Jenner** (1749-1823), the doctor who pioneered vaccination against smallpox. Jenner practised in Berkeley, Gloucestershire, and became interested in the country belief that those who had had cowpox were immune from smallpox. His researches, which at first aroused great opposition, interested the royal family; vaccination gradually spread through England and Parliament voted Jenner a grant of £10,000. Jenner's statue was first erected in Trafalgar Square in 1858 but was sent to Kensington Gardens in 1862. There was argument about the site; *Punch* could not resist:

> England ...
> I saved you many million
>   spots,
> And now you grudge one spot
>   to me!

Turn directly away from the Jenner statue to see a granite obelisk in memory of **John Hanning Speke** (1827-64), the African explorer who discovered the source of the Nile. Speke was due to address the meeting of the British Association in Bath but carelessly shot himself while partridge shooting on the morning of the meeting. His former companion on African travels, James Grant, was writing his account of their expedition when he was told of

Right: *Forgotten today but remembered in Kensington Gardens, John Hanning Speke was famous for discovering Lake Victoria Nyanza.*

Speke's death. He had the pages he was writing at the time published with a black border.

One of London's most popular statues, in *art nouveau* style with mice, rabbits, squirrels and fairies, is **Peter Pan**, by Sir George Frampton (1911), which stands on the west bank of Long Water and is one of the rare statues in London to a modern fictional character. *Peter Pan*, Sir James Barrie's play, was first produced on 27th December 1904 with Nina Boucicault (who modelled for this statue) as the first Peter Pan. He, Nana the dog-nurse, Tinker Bell, Wendy, Captain Hook and other characters remain an inseparable part of nursery life. Despite early scepticism the play proved to be an instant success and has been produced annually ever since.

Barrie himself commissioned the statue and unofficially arranged with the first Commissioner of Works to have it erected. When this was discovered a question was asked in Parliament but the statue was so clearly an attraction that it was not disturbed. While

In Kensington Gardens is 'Physical Energy' by G. F. Watts, who at the age of 47 married the sixteen-year-old Ellen Terry.

adults may find fault, the high gloss on the rabbits' ears points to generations of loving caresses from children's hands. The sculptor's own memorial in St Paul's shows a figure holding a model of the Peter Pan statue.

A little to the south of Peter Pan is a bronze 12 foot equestrian figure, **Physical Energy** (1907), the *chef d'oeuvre* of G. F. Watts. It is a replica of part of the memorial to Cecil Rhodes at Groote Schuur, near Cape Town.

The Broad Walk runs from north to south of Kensington Gardens and Kensington Palace is on its left. On the south side of the Palace in the Gardens is a statue of **William III** presented to Edward VII in 1907 by Emperor William II of Germany. Between the Palace and the Broad Walk is a white marble statue (1893) of **Queen Victoria** by her daughter Princess Louise (1848-1939). The princess, a sculptor of considerable talent whose royal position deprived her of her rightful place in British sculpture, was taught by Sir Joseph Edgar Boehm and in 1890 the princess had the unpleasant experience of finding her tutor dead in his studio.

On the north side of Holland Park, Kensington, on a plinth in the centre of a small pond is a bronze statue by G. F. Watts and Edgar Boehm, of **Henry Fox, 3rd Baron Holland** (1773-1840), nephew of Charles James Fox. He is seated and holds a stick: in life he suffered badly from gout. Henry Holland was an aristocratic radical, internationally minded, pro-French, opposed to slavery and 'perhaps the greatest host in English history'. He had political ambitions but when he was a possible candidate for the post of Foreign Secretary it is said that Lord John Russell had the delicate task of explaining to him that, to a man, the Cabinet flatly refused to work with a man

This marble statue of Queen Victoria was made by her gifted daughter, Princess Louise.

At the junction of Holland Park and Holland Park Avenue, across the road from Holland Park underground station, is the statue of **St Volodymyr the Great, Prince of Rus** (960-1015), founder of Christianity in Russia. Volodymyr was raised a pagan but after reflection decided that unification of his peoples could only come through a common religion. Comparison led him to choose the Orthodox Church and he ordered the people of Kiev (the capital) to be baptised. Enlightenment prevailed: Volodymyr abolished capital punishment and built a new life for his country based on Christian ritual and churchbuilding. 1988 marked the completion of 1,000 years of Christianity in Russia and the Orthodox Church unveiled this statue by Leonard Mol on 29th May to mark the occasion.

St Volodymyr the Great was the founder of Christianity in Russia.

whose wife opened his letters! Lady Holland (of whom Macaulay said: 'She has the air of Queen Elizabeth') was known as both beautiful and masterful. Denied his wish, Holland took revenge by operating a species of alternative foreign service from Holland House, supporting the unconventional, the liberal and the progressive. His salons were brilliant: 'the favourite resort', Macaulay wrote, 'of wits and beauties, painters and poets, scholars, philosophers and statesmen.' Last words can be great indices to character. Lord Holland's were: 'If Mr Selwyn calls, let him in; if I am alive I shall be very glad to see him, and if I am dead he will be very glad to see me.'

Holland House was damaged by incendiary bombs during the Second World War but when Lord Ilchester finally sold it to the London County Council in 1952 the purchaser was placed under an obligation 'to maintain the statue of Lord Holland'. It has been faithfully observed.

Left: *President Roosevelt's statue in Grosvenor Square shows FDR in his familiar cloak.*

Below: *General Eisenhower's statue in Grosvenor Square, 'Little America', where John Adams, first minister to Great Britain, had his residence.*

» 9 «
OXFORD STREET, MAYFAIR, REGENT STREET, SOHO

Until 1851 **Marble Arch** was the entrance to Buckingham Palace and had been set up in 1828 at a cost of £80,000 by John Nash: Chantrey's statue of George IV (now in Trafalgar Square) was destined to crown it but was never put up. The Arch was intended to symbolise the victories of Trafalgar and Waterloo but the conception altered and the panels represent the Spirit of England inspiring Youth, Valour and Virtue and Peace and Plenty. The sculptors were Flaxman, Westmacott, Rossi and Baily and the superb bronze gates were made by Samuel Parker.

At the junction of Bayswater Road and Oxford Street stood the **Tyburn** gallows for nearly 600 years. Public executions, to which the condemned (who included Perkin Warbeck and Jack Sheppard) were brought by cart from Newgate prison and the Tower, took place here at a spot now marked by a stone in the traffic island at the end of Edgware Road. Popular executions attracted enormous crowds: 200,000 are supposed to have attended Sheppard's hanging, and Jonathan Wild created a great sensation by succeeding in picking the hangman's pocket as he adjusted the noose!

Grosvenor Square lies south of Oxford Street. It was first laid out by Sir Richard Grosvenor (ancestor of the Duke of Westminster) in 1695 and is one of the earliest examples of landscaping of this type. The Square has been nicknamed 'Little America'. The association began early when John Adams, later President, moved here in 1785 and by the Second World War the Square was surrounded by American offices and institutions. Now the name is even more merited with Saarinen's vast embassy surmounted by a gilded eagle with a wing span of 35 feet. The statue of **President Franklin Delano Roosevelt** (1882-1945) was erected in 1948. The sculptor was Sir William Reid Dick and it was unveiled by Mrs Roosevelt on 12th April 1948, the third anniversary of the President's death. The subscription list was open to British subscribers only and contributions were limited to 5 shillings (25p) per person. 200,000 contributed to the fund and the sum required was raised within 24 hours. An avenue of trees leads to the statue, which is flanked by fountains and shows the President cloaked and leaning on a stick.

The statue of **Dwight David Eisenhower** (1890-1969), US general, commander of Allied forces in the invasion of Europe, Republican statesman and President of the United States, stands near Number 20, his wartime headquarters.

The US Ambassador to Britain, Charles H. Price, and Mrs Price had noticed the lack of a statue of the wartime chief and raised funds among friends and associates in Kan-

The Earl of Chatham's second son, William Pitt the Younger, became Prime Minister at 24 and was in office during the Napoleonic Wars.

sas City (in which locality Eisenhower had been raised) to pay for it. It is by the American sculptor Robert Dean and was unveiled by Margaret Thatcher, Prime Minister, and Charles H. Price on 23rd January 1989. Eisenhower is shown in uniform, in relaxed stance, hands on hips. On the marble surround is a chronology of the general's career and on the reverse the historic Order of the Day for 6th June 1944, D-Day.

Eisenhower was Commander of Allied Forces in North Africa, 1942-3; Supreme Allied Commander Europe, 1943-5; Chief of Staff, American Army, 1945; First Military Commander of NATO, 1950-2; and President of the United States, 1952-60. His presidency saw the ending of the Korean War and the signing into law of the Civil Rights Act. He was that rarest of presidents, one whose personal popularity was nearly as great on retirement as it was on the day he was elected.

Also here is the **American Eagle Squadrons' Memorial** (1986) to those Americans who volunteered to fight for Britain before the United States joined the Second World War.

From the north- east corner of Grosvenor Square, Brook Street leads to and crosses Davies Street, south of which is Berkeley Square. Here is a white marble **Nymph** with reeds and a pitcher-fountain (not used for many years). It is the work of Alexander Munro (1825-71) and was presented by Henry, 3rd Marquess of Lansdowne, who lived nearby in Lansdowne House.

Brook Street continues on to Hanover Square, at the south end of which, facing the fashionable St George's Church, is a bronze statue of **William Pitt the Younger** (1759-1806), the British statesman and Prime Minister, by Sir Francis Legatt Chantrey. The statue had a stormy early life and was nearly removed by the Whigs when first put up in 1831. George III had a great liking for Pitt (called the 'Great Commoner') and when Pitt resumed office in 1804 he congratulated the king on looking in better health than when they had last met in 1801. 'That is not to be wondered at,' replied the king. 'I was then on the point of parting with an old friend: I am now about to regain one!' One of history's most extraordinary discrepancies occurs in the two versions of Pitt's alleged last words on his death bed in 1806: one observer reported them as 'My country! Oh my country!' but another (more practically) as: 'I think I could eat one of Bellamy's veal pies!'

Due north from Hanover Square, across Oxford Street, is Cavendish Square, which dates from 1717. It has a bronze statue of **Lord William George Frederick Bentinck** (1802-48), made in 1848 by T. Campbell and erected in 1851. Bentinck was a politician, secretary to his uncle Canning and a great sportsman who became leader of the Protectionist party and opponent to Peel. He is shown in a frock coat with a cloak over his shoulder.

Cavendish Place leads to Langham Place. **John Nash** (1752-1835), the architect, is remembered at his church of All Souls, Langham Place, with a wall-bust by Cecil Thomas under the portico. It was unveiled in 1956. Nash built All Souls' to close the vista and complete his grand scheme for Regent Street, 1823-4. His simple needle-like spire, much admired today, was derided by Nash's contemporaries. After a Parliamentary debate in which the spire was sharply criticised and a cartoon was published showing Nash impaled on it by the seat of his trousers, he rather relished the publicity and, refusing to be depressed, joked with his assistants: 'See, gentlemen, how criticism has exalted me!'

No one had greater influence on the appearance of the London of his day. The agreeable effects are still to be seen in Nash's many London buildings. The gleaming

Nash's smile enhances one of his most admired buildings, All Souls' Church, Langham Place.

Quintin Hogg's achievements included founding the Regent Street Polytechnic and his statue in Portland Place is close to it.

white stucco façades and Corinthian columns of Carlton House Terrace (1827-32) make it the most inspiring of Nash's works. Nash popularised stucco, a paste based on a powder of fired clay nodules from the Isle of Sheppey, which looked like stone but was vastly cheaper. The wits were quick to extemporise:

Augustus at Rome was for building
   renown'd,
And of marble he left whàt of brick he
   had found.
But is not our Nash, too, a very great
   master?
He finds us all brick and he leaves us all
   plaster!

In Portland Place (at the southern end, close to All Souls') is a monument to the philanthropist **Quintin Hogg** (1845-1903), founder of the Regent Street Polytechnic in 1882. The statue, erected in 1906, is by Sir George Frampton RA, who was knighted in

1908, and shows Hogg surrounded by a group of boys, one of whom holds a football. Hogg lived at 5 Cavendish Square and founded the Polytechnic to provide day and evening technical instruction for students. Practically, he also organised cheap holidays abroad for members and helped them obtain jobs. In 1902 the government implemented Hogg's idea and founded labour bureaux in the metropolitan boroughs at public expense.

Further north along Portland Place is the bronze equestrian statue of **Sir George White** (1835-1912), defender of Ladysmith, by John Tweed, 1922.

Here too is **Lord Lister** (1827-1912), the surgeon and pioneer of the antiseptic method of surgery. He lived at Park Crescent and his statue by Sir Thomas Brock is sited near his old home. Lister developed an early interest in gangrene and inflammation, studied and developed carbolic acid as an anti-

Elected in 1960, John Kennedy was the youngest President in the history of the United States. His bust faces Marylebone Road.

septic and published his findings in *The Lancet* in 1867. His techniques revolutionised surgical operations: he became the first medical peer and one of the twelve original members of the Order of Merit.

In Park Crescent at the end of Portland Place is a statue by Sebastian Gahagan of **Edward Augustus, Duke of Kent** (1767-1820), father of Queen Victoria, his only child. Gahagan, an Irishman and a pupil and follower of Nollekens, had great talent. His first Academy exhibit appeared in 1802.

The International Students' Hostel built in 1965 at 1 Park Crescent (at the corner of Marylebone Road) has a memorial bust of **President John Fitzgerald Kennedy** (born in 1917 and assassinated in 1963). Mr Kennedy was the youngest President of the United States ever to be elected and specially associated himself with social reform and the civil rights movement.

West along the Marylebone Road, at the corner of Marylebone High Street, opposite the Royal Academy of Music was the house which was the home of **Charles Dickens** from 1839 to 1851. *The Old Curiosity Shop, Barnaby Rudge, Martin Chuzzlewit, David Copperfield* and the *Christmas Carol* were written here and on the wall of

The Duke of Kent (1767-1820), father of Queen Victoria, died eight months after her birth. He stands at the north end of Portland Place.

Left: *George II in Golden Square was the last British monarch to command in battle.*
Right: *This weathered statue of Charles II once belonged to W. S. Gilbert. It was erected in Soho Square in 1938.*

Ferguson House is a sculptured panel with a portrait of Dickens. Although *Dombey and Son* was largely written in Switzerland it draws many of its scenes from this neighbourhood and the church where Paul Dombey was christened and Mr Dombey married has been identified as St Marylebone.

Further to the west, at 1 Dorset Square, was the office of the **Free French** forces engaged in resistance work. A moving plaque unveiled in 1957 notes that it was placed 'to commemorate the deeds of the men and women of the Free French Forces and their British comrades who left from this house on special missions to enemy-occupied France'. Sadly, many of them did not return.

South of Oxford Street, in the centre of Soho Square is a weathered statue of **Charles II** by Caius Gabriel Cibber (1630-

1700), the son of the actor-dramatist Colley Cibber. This Danish sculptor, who came to England and worked at Chatsworth for the 4th Earl of Devonshire (under whom he fought for William of Orange, who made him Royal Carver), was also responsible for the bas-reliefs on the Monument and for the phoenix on St Paul's.

Golden Square, also in Soho, is south of Carnaby Street, east of Regent Street. It has a statue of **George II** (1683-1760) with hand extended in a welcoming gesture, by John Nost the Elder, made in 1720 and erected here in 1753. Dickens wrote of this 'mournful statue, the guardian genius of a little wilderness of shrubs'. In his way the king was a tactful husband for when Queen Caroline, as she lay dying, urged him to marry again he replied, 'Non, j'aurai des maîtresses', to which the queen briskly replied, 'Ah, mon Dieu, cela n'empêche pas'.

Captain Coram, who died in 1751, would be happy to know that his Foundation still flourishes in London and Hertfordshire.

» 10 «
BLOOMSBURY AND NORTHWARDS

On the south side of Russell Square, facing down Bedford Place, is a statue of **Francis Russell, 5th Duke of Bedford** (1765-1805), the great agriculturalist, builder of the square and a large landowner in this area (the name Russell is the family name of the Dukes of Bedford). The statue, by Westmacott (1809), shows the Duke with his hand on a plough with sheep at his feet and four cherubs representing the four seasons. Winter is shown well muffled up.

At Number 30 Russell Square is the Royal Institute of Chemistry, built in 1915, with a seated statue by Gilbert Bayes of **Joseph Priestley** (1733-1804), the nonconformist minister who discovered oxygen and did valuable research into other gases.

In Bloomsbury Square, facing Great Russell Street, is a statue of **Charles James Fox** (1749-1806), the statesman, an ardent Whig who passionately defended the liberties of the individual and 'one of the most charming men of any age'. The statue is by Sir Richard Westmacott (1816) and Fox sits with a copy of the *Magna Carta* in his hand. He did everything with enormous concentration. Even relaxation was amongst his talents and he would sit for hours against the garden wall of his home at St Anne's Hill, doing nothing. 'Ah, Mr Fox,' said a friend to him, 'how delightful it must be to loll along in the sun at your ease with a book in your hand.' 'Why the book? why the book?' was the reply. Perhaps some of Fox's power over his audiences arose from his sensible rules for speech-making:

'no Greek, as much Latin as you like, and *never* French under any circumstances'. Bloomsbury Square dates from 1665 and is one of the oldest squares in London and indeed the first open space in London to be given the name 'square'.

In Great Russell Street at Congress House, the headquarters of the Trades Union Congress, the permanent association of British trades unions, is an impressive **war memorial sculpture to trade unionists** by Sir Jacob Epstein (1958) cut from a solid 10 ton block of Roman stone and set off by a green Carrara marble background.

St George's Church in Bloomsbury Way has a steeple surmounted by an extraordinary statue, erected by a loyal brewer, of **George I** as St George (and described by Horace Walpole as a 'master-stroke of absurdity'). The church was built by Hawksmoor in 1716-45 and this incongruous figure of the king in Roman dress gave rise to many jokes and to the rhyme:

When Harry the Eighth left the Pope in the lurch,
He ruled over England as head of the church,
But George's good subjects, the Bloomsbury people,
Instead of the church, made him head of the steeple!

George's views on sculptors are not recorded but he did once say, in his heavy German accent, 'I hate all Boets and Bainters'!

Near the junction of Southampton Row

and Holborn at the former Baptist Church House is a statue of **John Bunyan** (1628-88) put up in 1903 at the Catton Street corner of the building. Amongst Bunyan's many books is *Pilgrim's Progress*, which was partly written in Bedford jail, where Bunyan was imprisoned for unlawful preaching.

In Bloomsbury Square Charles James Fox holds a copy of Magna Carta.

John Bunyan's statue at Baptist Church House, Holborn, holds a book with the opening lines of 'Pilgrim's Progress'.

Catton Street leads to Procter Street and Red Lion Square. On the east side of the square, among the plane trees, is a bust of **Bertrand Arthur William Russell, 3rd Earl Russell** (1872-1970), by Marcelle Quinton (1980). Russell, the greatest British rationalist philosopher, logician, mathematician and political campaigner of the twentieth century, had a profound influence on modern thought. He wrote widely and

vigorously and was honoured with the Order of Merit in 1948 and the Nobel Prize for Literature in 1950. Today he is perhaps most generally remembered for his support of the Campaign for Nuclear Disarmament. Something of a sensation was caused by the publication of his *Autobiography* (three volumes, 1967-9) which threw fresh light on his unhappy childhood and first marriage (he was married three times) and his relationship with Lady Ottoline Morrell and others.

Bertrand Russell, philosopher, contemplates Red Lion Square.

On the west side of Red Lion Square is a statue of **Fenner Brockway, Baron Brockway** (1888-1988), unveiled on 25th July 1985 by Michael Foot, watched by a jubilant Brockway, aged 96 and one of very few to have a statue erected in their lifetime. It is by Ian Walters, also responsible for the large bust of Nelson Mandela on the South Bank. Brockway was a conscientious objector in the First World War: he was a pacifist, pro-disarmament, anti-imperialist and a human rights activist. A Labour Party member, he was MP for Eton and Slough 1950-64, and then became a life peer. In 1987 the statue was hit by a falling tree and an arm broken off. The damage was repaired. Plans for the statue came from Liberation (formerly the Movement for Colonial Freedom), founded by Brockway in 1954. The Greater London Council was a major contributor to the statue fund.

Queen Square at the west end of Great Ormond Street has a statue of about 1775, which may be **Queen Charlotte, Queen Anne** or **Mary II**, although most probably Charlotte.

North of Queen Square, Guilford Street runs east to Brunswick Square. At Number 40 are the offices of the Thomas Coram Foundation, once known as the Foundling Hospital. This was started in 1739 by the warm-hearted **Captain Thomas Coram** (1668-1751), who was distressed by the sight of 'deserted infants exposed to the inclemencies of the season' in the streets of London. Outside is a statue of Coram by William Macmillan (1953) in a pose taken from Hogarth's portrait of the Captain. In the early days of the hospital Hogarth painted this portrait and persuaded fellow artists including Gainsborough, Kneller, Rysbrack and Roubillac to present works of art to aid the funds and the resulting art gallery be-

came a fashionable rendezvous for London society in the reign of George II. In 1749 Handel gave a performance of his own works which raised 500 guineas for the hospital and every year his *Messiah* was sung in the chapel there. Over the years the performances raised over £7,000 for the maintenance of Coram's work.

The animated pose of Fenner Brockway's statue reflects the fact that Brockway was still living when it was erected, and even saw it unveiled.

Hunter Street runs north from Brunswick Square. Leigh Street to the west leads to Cartwright Gardens, where a bronze statue by George Clarke (1831) of **Major John Cartwright** (1740-1824) stands in the gardens named after him. He was the brother of Edmund Cartwright, inventor of the power loom, and helped with the business aspects of the invention. The plinth tells of John's own campaigns for universal

suffrage, equal representation and vote by ballot in annual parliaments modelled on the Anglo-Saxon folk-meets. This was strong medicine and not without repercussions. At the age of 81 John Cartwright escaped conviction for sedition by the smallest of margins but was heavily fined instead.

In the courtyard of the British Medical Association on the east side of Tavistock Square (the eldest son of the Duke of Bedford takes the title of Marquess of Tavistock) is a fountain by James Woodford and S. Rowland Pierce, which was dedicated in 1954 to **British medical men and women** who died in the Second World War.

At the south-east corner of the square itself is a memorial to **Dame Louisa Brandreth Aldrich-Blake** (1865-1925), the surgeon, by Sir Edwin Lutyens with a double bust by A. G. Walker. Dame Louisa is described in the *Dictionary of National Biography* as 'distinguished for her skill in boxing and cricket, at that date unusual in a girl'.

Above: *Major John Cartwright, a free spirit, was lucky to escape prison for his views. His statue is at home among students' halls of residence in Cartwright Gardens near Euston.*

Right: *Two busts, back to back, are an unusual feature of Louisa Aldrich-Blake's memorial in Tavistock Square.*

In Tavistock Square, the figure of Gandhi, erected in 1968, is seated on a hollow box which holds flowers and wreaths.

In the centre of the square is **Mohandas Karamchand Gandhi** (1869-1948), the principal creator of India's independence. He is better known as Mahatma (Saint)

Robert Stephenson, whose statue stands at Euston station, was Chief Engineer of the London to Birmingham Railway.

Gandhi and is depicted here in the position of prayer.

Euston was the London terminus of the London to Birmingham Railway opened in 1838 and a statue of its Chief Engineer, **Robert Stephenson,** by Baron Marochetti, was moved from Euston Square to the fore-court of the rebuilt Euston station in 1968. Stephenson would have taken the greatest professional interest in this piece of new railway planning 130 years after his great work. Stephenson, one of the group of great nineteenth-century engineers, took a part in helping to construct his father George Stephenson's famous locomotive *Rocket* in 1827 and became one of the outstanding figures of early railway history. He was also MP for Whitby from 1847 to 1848. A contemporary wrote enthusiastically: 'Robert Stephenson may be regarded as a type and pattern of the onward-moving English race, practical, scientific, energetic and in the hour of trial, heroic.'

Further north, in Camden High Street, is a statue of **Richard Cobden** (1804-65), the statesman and economist and an outstanding figure in the Anti-Corn Law League. The Corn Laws of 1815 ordained that grain could not be imported into Great Britain until the domestic price had reached £4 a quarter. This, coupled with bad harvests, caused great hardship. In 1836 agitation began in Manchester for the repeal of these iniquitous laws and two years later the Anti-Corn Law League was formed. The further disaster of the Irish famine of 1846 con-verted Peel and Russell to Cobden's views, the Corn Laws were repealed and Cobden was hailed as the 'Saviour of the Poor'. The statue, which still stands on its original site, is 8 feet high and of Sicilian marble. It was unveiled in July 1868 amidst scenes of the wildest rejoicing.

» 11 «
PADDINGTON, ST JOHN'S WOOD AND NORTHWARDS TO HIGHGATE

Facing Bayswater Road is Orme Square, which was built about 1815 and named after Mr Orme, the Bond Street printseller who bought the ground. A column surmounted by an eagle stands here to commemorate the triumphal visit of the Tsar and the Allied sovereigns to England in 1815 after Napoleon's defeat at Waterloo. Close by are other reminders: Moscow Road, Coburgh Place and St Petersburgh Place.

In Paddington station, the principal railway terminus for the west of England from the grand days of the Great Western Railway (GWR or God's Wonderful Railway to its many admirers) to the more utilitarian administration of British Rail, sits the statue of **Isambard Kingdom Brunel** (1806-59), also remembered on the Embankment. The Paddington statue, by John Doubleday, was presented to BR Western Region by the Bristol & West Building Society and was unveiled by the Lord Mayor of Westminster in 1982. Brunel was a brilliant engineer. He was also a romantic.

Isambard Kingdom Brunel, once Chief Engineer of the Great Western Railway, surveys Paddington station from a seat at the top of the stairs to the Underground.

He arranged the alignment of Box Tunnel, Bath, at 1³/₄ miles the longest in England when first built, so that the sun shone through it on his birthday, 9th April.

On Paddington Green is a white marble statue of **Mrs Sarah Siddons**, the actress (1755-1831), who is buried at the north end of the churchyard of St Mary's Church, now a recreation ground. The statue by Léon-Joseph Chavalliaud was erected in 1897 and unveiled by the actor Sir Henry Irving. It was inspired by Sir Joshua Reynolds's painting 'The Tragic Muse'. After a period in the provinces Sarah Siddons came to London in 1782 where she was a tremendous success and drew huge crowds until her retirement in 1812. Although she failed in comedy she was a brilliant tragedian and the statue shows her in a characteristic pose. She was eagerly painted by all the leading portraitists of her day but Thomas Gainsborough at least seems to have experienced some difficulty for while painting her portrait he is said to have thrown down his brush with the angry remark: 'Dammit, madam, there is no end to your nose.' 5,000 people attended her funeral, which was the most spectacular ever seen in Paddington.

At Lord's Cricket Ground, St John's Wood, headquarters of the MCC, the main entrance gates, designed by Sir Herbert Baker, are a memorial (1923) to the legendary **W. G. Grace** (1848-1915). Grace played 44 seasons of first-class cricket, made 54,896 runs, took 2,876 wickets and made 126 centuries. At the same time he was a doctor with a busy practice in Bristol. On the gates' central pillar are the initials WGG, above them a set of stumps and bails with a ball below and a bat on either side. A lion supervises these items. Perhaps this is the place to remember WGG's imperturbability under fire. In 1896 Ernest Jones, the Australian fast bowler, bowled straight through Grace's magnificent beard. The master merely called out: 'Whatever are you at?'

A copy of the Muse which the sculptor himself designed for his Shelley monument in University College Chapel, Oxford, accompanies a bust by A. C. Lacchesi, to form the monument at the junction of Abbey Road and Grove End Road, to **Edward Onslow Ford** RA (1852-1901). The Muse holds a broken-stringed lyre and the inscription reads: 'To thyself be true.' The monument was erected in 1903 by friends and admirers. The inscription is puzzling. It may be a misquotation of Hamlet's 'To thine own self be true' or, more probably, a reference to Sarah Bolton's famous poem in *Harper's Magazine*, 1854:

Voyage upon life's sea,
To yourself be true
And, what'er your lot may be,
Paddle your own canoe.

Sigmund Freud, the eminent psycho-analyst (1856-1939), lived at 20 Maresfield

Gardens, NW3, his home after he had fled from Nazi Austria to London in 1938. Despite the pressures of flight he had brought with him furniture, books and financial resources and he reconstructed his Vienna study in London, where it became a meeting-place for psychoanalysts.

Freud was nearing the end of a distinguished career. He had been professor of neurology at Vienna University 1902-38. He wrote and lectured widely. In London he devoted himself to *Moses and Monotheism*, a dissertation supporting, through psychoanalysis, the theory that Moses was Egyptian. Freud was fearful that this would be seen as an attack on Judaism (a sensitive issue) but it was acclaimed by the British Psychoanalytical Society on 10th March 1939, a far cry from the hostility that had greeted his early work. Sadly it was nearly too late. Freud had suffered from cancer since 1923 and died on 23rd September 1939. He was seeing patients only weeks before his death.

Freud's statue, by Oscar Nemon, stands by Swiss Cottage Library, facing Adelaide Road. It was unveiled on 2nd October 1970 by three of Freud's great-grandchildren.

At the Zoo end of the Broad Walk, Regent's Park, stands the **Parsee Fountain**, a 16 foot fountain of granite and marble (1869), decorated, inevitably, with a marble head of Queen Victoria. It was the gift of a wealthy Parsee of Bombay, Sir Cowasjeen Jehangir, 'a token of gratitude to the people of England for the protection enjoyed by him and his Parsee fellow countrymen under the British rule in India'. At one time there was a waterclock as well but this broke down and was removed. Sir Cowasjeen's gratitude perhaps had its roots in the history of his people, disciples of Zoroaster, paying homage to the sun and fire, and descendants of those who had fled from Persia to India to escape Moslem persecution. By the nineteenth century they formed a small, wealthy group of merchants, largely in Bombay.

The painter and sculptor **Sigismund Christian Hubert Goetz** (1866-1939) did much to adorn Regent's Park and the mermaid fountain in Queen Mary's Gardens there, which is the work of William Macmillan, commemorates him.

Further north at Waterlow Park, a fine open space on Highgate Hill, once the garden of **Sir Sydney Waterlow's** house, which he gave, together with the estate of about 30 acres, to London County Council in 1889, is a statue by Frank M. Taubman (1900), of Sir Sydney in which he is shown sensibly carrying his umbrella with a soft hat in one hand and

Sir Sydney Waterlow's statue stands on the site of his former home in Highgate.

his key in the other. Sir Sydney, 1st baronet (1822-1906), was Lord Mayor of London and Master of the Stationers' Company.

At the foot of Highgate Hill, near Salisbury Walk is the **Whittington Stone**, a memorial to another Lord Mayor of London. This stone, said to be the third placed on the site, marks the spot where Dick Whittington is said to have sat with his cat to hear Bow bells ringing out 'Turn again, Whittington, thrice Mayor of London Town'. The figure of the cat was added in 1964. The origins of the legend about him are now obscure but Whittington is known to have been a mercer, immensely rich in later life, lending money successively to Richard II, Henry IV and Henry V, and Lord Mayor of London in 1397, 1406 and 1419.

Beribboned wreaths of red flowers left by enthusiasts adorn the monument to **Heinrich Karl Marx** (1818-83) in Highgate Cemetery. Who knows how long they may continue to do so? The colossal, leonine, bearded, bronze bust, four times life-size, sculpted by Lawrence Bradshaw (1956), commemorates this socialist thinker who lived in London and spent the last 27 years of his life in St Pancras. Quotations from Marxist dogma, 'Workers of all lands unite', from the *Communist Manifesto* of 1848 (the year of revolution), and 'The philosophers have only interpreted the world in various ways, the point, however, is to change it', decorate the plinth. Until cemetery replanning in 1956 the Marx family was commemorated by a plain slab only.

Left: *Samuel Johnson's statue at St Clement Danes, where he attended services, faces down Fleet Street.*

Below: *James Boswell's 'Life of Samuel Johnson' was a brilliant portrait. A panel on Johnson's statue shows Johnson and Boswell together.*

Left: *Dour yet popular, Gladstone inspired this pub song, 'God bless the people's William, Long may he lead the van, Of Liberty and Freedom, God bless the Grand Old Man!'*

Facing page: *Count Peter of Savoy's gilt bronze statue stands over the Savoy Hotel's entrance.*

» 12 «
STRAND TO BANK, ALDWYCH,
LINCOLN'S INN

Somerset House in the Strand, by the north end of Waterloo Bridge, has in its forecourt a notable statue of **George III** by John Bacon the Elder which stands on a foundation in the quadrangle, showing the king leaning on a ship's rudder with a lion, ship's prow and Neptune as companions.

At Aldwych on the north entrance to Bush House, facing up Kingsway, is a group of two huge figures of **Youth**, by the American Malvina Hoffman, put up in 1925 to symbolise the friendship between Britain and the United States of America: they are dedicated 'to the Friendship of the English-Speaking Peoples'. Bush House was constructed by an American syndicate and completed in 1931 to the designs of Helmle, Corbett and Harrison of New York and named after Irving T. Bush, the American business executive. This symbolic sculpture was unveiled by the Earl of Balfour.

Over the Strand entrance of the Savoy Hotel stands the

gilt bronze figure of **Count Peter of Savoy** (1303-68), in medieval dress with a shield and a 14 foot spear. It is by Frank Lynn Jenkins, an American, and was erected in 1904. Henry III gave the site to Peter, Earl of Savoy and Richmond, uncle of Henry's wife, Eleanor of Provence, and brother of Boniface, Archbishop of Canterbury, for an annual rent of three barbed arrows. Here in 1346 he built the magnificent Savoy Palace. When Peter died he left the property to the Great St Bernard Hospice in Savoy but Eleanor bought it back two years later. Very much later, the Savoy Hotel, which itself dates from 1903-10 and was the work of T. E. Collcutt and A. H. Macmurdo, was built on the site. The Savoy Theatre, forever linked with the Gilbert and Sullivan operas, is reached from the hotel forecourt.

In 1989 a **sundial** in a lead tub was set up in Savoy Gardens, between the hotel and the river, to commemorate the centenary of the Savoy Theatre, the D'Oyly Carte family who financed it and others connected with the hotel.

Outside St Clement Danes, the RAF's own church at the east end of the Strand, stands the statue of Air Chief Marshal **Hugh Dowding, 1st Baron Dowding** (1882-1970), to whom Britain owed her victory in the battle of Britain, 1940. 'Stuffy' Dowding began service life in the Army, then joined the Royal Flying Corps and in 1918 the new Royal Air Force. From 1930 to 1935 he served on the Air Council as member for Supply, Research and Development. At this time technical advances which were to give Britain a vital edge in the battle were under development, including radar. In 1936 Dowding was appointed to the post of Commander-in-Chief Fighter Command which was to win him and his pilots the admiration of the nation. He began to build up a force of fast, manoeuvreable Hurricane and Spitfire fighter aircraft. In May 1940, when France was crumbling, the government was pressed to send RAF squadrons to France to stiffen a failing defence but Dowding, aware like Churchill that the battle of France was over and that the battle of Britain was about to begin, refused. His slim resources had to be preserved for the island's defence. The refusal did much to ensure British victory in July-October 1940. Many felt the statue to be long overdue.

Dowding's larger than life bronze statue, the campaign for which was led by the Battle of Britain Fighter Association, is by Faith Winter. It was unveiled on the sunny morning of 31st October 1988 by Queen Elizabeth the Queen Mother (herself resident in London during the battle) at 10.45 am and, exactly on time, a solitary Spitfire flew in salute overhead. Dowding is shown in uniform in a characteristic pose, thumbs hooked into breast pockets. His son Derek, himself a battle of Britain pilot, described the statue as 'an uncanny likeness'.

Also by Faith Winter, a 9 foot bronze statue of Marshal of the Royal Air Force **Sir Arthur Travers Harris**, 1st Baron (1892-1984), who was called upon by Portal in 1942 to be Commander-in-Chief Bomber Command, was unveiled here by Queen Elizabeth the Queen Mother on 31st May 1992. It shows Harris in uniform, in a contemplative pose, his hands linked behind him. Harris, who became known as 'Bomber' Harris, is remembered for the great raids on German cities such as Hamburg. There is no question that his steadfastness and the great gallantry of his bomber crews had a decisive effect on the outcome of the Second World War and made an outstanding contribution to Allied victory.

Lord Dowding's statue is outside the Royal Air Force church, St Clement Danes.

The bronze of Sir Arthur Harris is burnished by the sculptor, Faith Winter, who also created the bronze of Dowding.

Also near the west front of St Clement Danes is the **William Ewart Gladstone Memorial** by Sir William Hamo Thornycroft RA (1850-1925), which shows the statesman in the robes of Chancellor of the Exchequer with groups expressing Brotherhood, Education, Aspiration and Courage. The statue of this dour statesman and Prime Minister (not a favourite of Queen Victoria, who complained 'He speaks to Me as if I were a public meeting') was unveiled in 1905 by Lord Morley.

Gladstone (1809-98), a survivor, eventually nicknamed 'The Grand Old Man' of British politics, started life as a Conservative but moved to the Liberal party. Few statesmen could boast of a greater volume of successful legislation: his only real failure was in the matter of Home Rule for Ireland. Although a fluent writer on theological and political topics he is little read

today. His oratory may be better remembered. There is a timeless common sense, for example, in his words: 'All the world over, I will back the masses against the classes.' His name is forever linked with a certain shape of small briefcase he favoured and which took its name from his. And 'Gladstone' was the name once given to a cheap claret because, in 1860, when Chancellor of the Exchequer, he reduced the duty on French wines.

At the other end of St Clement Danes church, facing Fleet Street, is a bronze statue by Percy Fitzgerald (1910) of **Dr Samuel Johnson** (1709-84), 'critic, essayist, philologist, biographer, wit, poet, moralist, dramatist, political writer, talker', and a regular worshipper at the church. His home was nearby at 17 Gough Square. The house is open to the public and has many Johnsonian relics: you can see the attic where he and his six indefatigable assistants worked on the great *Dictionary*. Boswell's *Life of Johnson* describes the final day's work: Mr Millar, bookseller, undertook the publication of Johnson's *Dictionary*. When the messenger who carried the last sheet to Millar returned, Johnson asked him, 'Well, what did he say?' 'Sir', answered the messenger, 'he said, "Thank God I have done with him".' 'I am glad', replied Johnson, with a smile, 'that he thanks God for any thing.'

Johnson, called by Tobias Smollett 'The Great Cham of Literature', is shown reading a book, with other books at his feet, recalling his words: 'A man will turn over half a library to make one book.' His bulky figure, in bushy full-bottomed wig, vividly reflects his appearance in life. He was normally irredeemably untidy, with sagging stockings and an old wig burned to the network by reckless encounters with bedside candles. The only concession he made to fashion was to appear at the opening of his *Irene* at Drury Lane in a scarlet waistcoat with gold braid and a gold laced hat. (It is sad to report that the piece failed and Johnson, asked how he felt, said 'Like the Monument'.) Apart from this sartorial effort the doctor went his own way although the Thrales did try to tidy him for dinner parties in later years. The sculptor, himself a devoted Johnsonian, not only sculpted the statue but gave it and unveiled it as well, when a royal unveiling was cancelled on the death of Edward VII. **James Boswell**, Johnson's indispensable biographer, is commemorated, like his close friend **Mrs Hester Lynch Thrale**, in bronze medallions on the statue's base. One Johnsonian pronouncement is germane to all statue-fanciers: 'In lapidary inscriptions a man is not upon oath.'

Near the Law Courts (more formally the Royal Courts of Justice) is the **Temple Bar Memorial** (1880), surmounted by a dragon, the unofficial badge of the City of London. It stands on the site of the old Temple Bar gateway into the City. Was the choice of a dragon a sardonic jest? One might imagine the Victorians to be incapable of such flippancy. In classic mythology the dragon was a rapacious monster supposed to keep watch on gold mines and buried treasure. Approaching humans were torn to pieces and had their avarice thus effectively quenched. The memorial has statues of Victoria and Edward VII (as Prince of Wales) by Sir Joseph Edgar Boehm RA, appointed sculptor to the Queen. **The Dragon**, by Charles Birch, stands on a plinth with bronze reliefs including one depicting the last occasion when royalty passed through the old gate, in 1872 when Victoria and the Prince of Wales gave thanks at St Paul's for the Prince's recovery from typhoid. Until 1772 heads of

executed criminals were stuck on the iron spikes of the gate and interested visitors could hire a telescope for a halfpenny to get a better view of them. When the sovereign visits the City it is here that she stops to receive the symbolic sword as a token of submission from the Lord Mayor. She returns it before entering the City.

The old gateway, by Wren, too narrow for the press of Victorian traffic, was taken to Theobalds Park, Hertfordshire, in 1878 where it still stands in a rural setting. There are plans to bring it back to London, perhaps to Paternoster Square, near St Paul's.

Chancery Lane leads north from Fleet Street to Lincoln's Inn. **Canada Walk**, the north walk of Lincoln's Inn Fields, west of the Inn, was named to commemorate the establishment of the headquarters of the Royal Canadian Air Force here, 1940-5. Beside the commemorative plaque is a maple tree, the gift of the people of Ottawa, planted in 1945.

Nearby is the memorial seat to **Margaret Ethel MacDonald**, wife of James Ramsay MacDonald, Britain's first Labour Prime Minister. She died at their home, 3 Lincoln's Inn Fields, in 1911 and this is one of the rarer London monuments to a woman other than a queen. It shows Mrs MacDonald with a group of nine children in bronze. The sculptor was R. R. Goulden and the inscription is: 'She brought joy to those with whom and for whom she lived.'

In the north-east corner of the Fields is a stone plinth to **William Frederick Danvers Smith, 2nd Viscount Hambleden** (1868-1928), head of W. H. Smith and Son, the newsagents and booksellers. The company offices used to be at Strand House in nearby Portugal Street, and Smith was MP for the Strand from 1891 until 1910. His bust which surmounted the plinth has been removed.

Elizabeth I's statue at St Dunstan-in-the-West is a contender for the title 'oldest outdoor statue in London'.

In the south-west corner of the Fields is N. F. Boonham's bronze bust of **John Hunter** (1728-93), the founder of scientific surgery, erected in 1977 by the President and Council of the Royal College of Surgeons to mark the Silver Jubilee of Queen Elizabeth II and the College's long association with Lincoln's Inn.

At the corner of Casey Street and Serle Street, behind the Law Courts, is a stone statue of **Thomas More**, at first-floor level. It is by Robert Smith, 1886, and is inscribed: 'The faithful servant both of God and the King. Martyred 6th July 1535.'

On the north side of Fleet Street is the church of St Dunstan-in-the-West. Over the door is a figure of **Queen Elizabeth I** by William Kerwin (1586), a strong claimant for the title of oldest outdoor statue in London. This, with the statues of King Lud and his two sons, came from the Ludgate which once stood halfway up Ludgate Hill and

was demolished in 1760-1. Evelyn noted in his *Diary* that the statue escaped the Great Fire.

Also on the church, close to the street, is a bronze bust by Lady Scott (Lady Hilton Young) of **Alfred Charles William Harmsworth, Viscount Northcliffe** (1865-1922), the newspaper proprietor and founder of the *Daily Mail*, which was unveiled in 1930 by Lord Riddell.

North of Fleet Street is Fetter Lane, location of **John Wilkes** (1727-97), whose statue proclaims him 'A champion of English freedom'. He founded a weekly periodical, the *North Briton*, in 1762, to attack the government. (It was so named because Smollett conducted the *Briton* on behalf of Lord Bute.) After one violent attack on faults in the Treaty of Paris, Wilkes was imprisoned in the Tower of London under a general warrant but released in 1763. Such was the

Left: *The bust of Alfred Harmsworth, Lord Northcliffe, at St Dunstan-in-the-West in Fleet Street was the work of Lady Scott (1930).*

Right: *Thomas Power O'Connor, Irish journalist and politician, is opposite the old Daily Telegraph building, Fleet Street.*

J. B. Birch's Queen Victoria, at the north end of Blackfriars Bridge.

outcry that two years later such warrants were ruled illegal. Wilkes's outspoken championship of freedom secured valuable political rights. Newspapers might publish full proceedings of both Houses; legally elected members of Parliament could not be kept from the House for their political beliefs. Three times the electors of Middlesex returned Wilkes and three times he was denied his seat before this right was established. Finally, in 1774, he took his seat without opposition and in the same year was elected Lord Mayor of London.

Wilkes married an heiress much older than himself. A Hellfire Club member, his mixture of dissipation, low morals, wit and ability made him the darling of the mob and

in the streets 'Wilkes for Liberty!' was the cry. He might have led a revolution; in fact he was a thoughtful and fair-minded alderman and magistrate. His statue, by James Butler, unveiled on 31st October 1988, stands at the corner of Fetter Lane and New Fetter Lane. Wilkes's famous squint is clearly seen. Here we have the only cross-eyed statue in London.

On the outside of the old *News Chronicle* building, opposite the old *Daily Telegraph* offices, is a bronze bust of the Irish journalist and politician **Thomas Power O'Connor** (1848-1929), nicknamed 'T P', who entered Parliament for Galway in 1880 and became a prominent personality in the Parnell party.

Salisbury Square, which is a turning off the south side of Fleet Street, is dominated by the obelisk erected in 1833 to **Robert Waithman**, Lord Mayor 1823-4 and a member of Parliament, 'the friend of liberty in evil times'. The redeveloped square was dedicated in 1990 by Lord Mayor Sir Hugh Bidwell to mark the 800th anniversary of the mayoralty of the City of London (1189-1989).

On the north-west side of Ludgate Circus is a tablet with a relief portrait of **Edgar Wallace** (1875-1932), the crime novelist and journalist, best known for his books *Four Just Men* and *Sanders of the River*. The memorial, by F. Doyle-Jones, was erected in 1934 and bears the words: 'He knew wealth and poverty yet had walked with kings and kept his bearing. Of his talents he gave lavishly to Authorship — but to Fleet Street he gave his heart.'

On the north side of Blackfriars Bridge is an ugly statue of **Queen Victoria** by John Bell Birch, unveiled on 21st July 1896. There are said to be some 150 statues of Victoria in the world, forty of them in India.

» 13 «
VICTORIA EMBANKMENT FROM WESTMINSTER TO BLACKFRIARS

The Embankment was the crowning achievement in 1864-70 of the engineer Sir Joseph Bazalgette (1819-91). The heavy cost was met by a levy of 13 pence on all coal sold in the metropolitan area and the work entailed reclaiming land daily covered by the tides and building a river wall 8 feet thick. The official opening by the Prince of Wales and Princess Louise took place on 13th July 1870. There are magnificent views of the river from here, with Big Ben at one end and St Paul's at the other end of what must be one of the finest riverside walks in the world.

At the corner of Westminster Bridge is a great group of the British queen **Boadicea** in her chariot by Thomas Thornycroft (1902). Boadicea, who died AD 62, was described by the Greek historian Dio Cassius as 'tall, fine-eyed and tawny-haired' and was made joint heir (with Nero) by her dying husband Prasutagus, ruler of the Iceni in East Anglia. This arrangement resulted in insults and oppressions and the Iceni revolted, followed by southern tribes. Paulinus met the Britons on an unidentified battle site and nearly annihilated them, Boadicea took poison and the rebellion was over. Note that the statue lacks reins.

Next to Cannon Row police station is an important and long overdue memorial to those who fought against the Japanese in Burma 1943-4, with Major-General Orde Wingate's **Chindit Special Force,** operating under the most arduous and dangerous conditions behind Japanese lines. Four of the force won the Victoria Cross. The monument takes the form of a bronze *Chinthe* — the lion-like beast in Burmese mythology from which the Chindits took their name and insignia. Sadly, Wingate (1904-44) was killed in an air crash before the war ended. The architect for the memorial was David Price; the sculptor, Frank Forster. It was unveiled by the Duke of Edinburgh on 10th October 1990.

'Father of the Royal Air Force' is a popular name for **Hugh Montague Trenchard,** 1st Viscount (1873-1956), whose statue by William Macmillan RA (1961) stands further along, in front of the former Air Ministry. More familiarly his nickname was 'Boom', a reference to his explosive and forceful speech. Trenchard began in the Army but in 1913 learned to fly (at the age of 39) and rose to command the Royal Flying Corps in the First World War. His was the inspiration for the innovative reconnaissance and bombing sorties. On 1st April 1918 the Royal Air Force was formed; Trenchard was the first Chief of Air Staff in 1919 and built up the new service, not without opposition from Army and Navy. He realised that he was dealing with 'a new breed of fighting men grappling with unknown forces in the loneliest element of all'.

Above: *Boadicea in her chariot was erected in 1902 by Westminster Bridge.*

When Trenchard retired he began a third successful career as Commissioner of the Metropolitan Police (1931-5) and founded the Hendon Police College. He was created Viscount in 1936. His statue shows him in uniform, with greatcoat and sword.

The Chindit Special Force monument (above), by Cannon Row police station, and a relief medallion of the Chindits' legendary leader, Major-General Orde Wingate (right), which appears at the back of the memorial.

As Chief of Air Staff throughout the Second World War, **Charles Frederick Algernon Portal, Viscount Portal of Hungerford**, Marshal of the Royal Air Force (1893-1971), fought his war at the great Anglo-American conferences and in Whitehall, where his statue (1975) by Oscar Nemon now stands on the lawns of the Ministry of Defence. It was unveiled by Harold Macmillan in 1975. Not only did the day-to-day supervision of the RAF fall to Portal but also the decisions on strategic plans, priorities and allocations. Portal reckoned that he had attended nearly 2,000 chiefs of staff meetings, 'each taking $1\frac{1}{2}$ to 2 hours or more and needing 3 or 4 hours of reading beforehand'. His stature is plainly declared by the judgements of wartime colleagues. Arthur 'Bomber' Harris said: 'Anything you could do, Peter Portal could do better'; Eisenhower: 'Greater even than Churchill'; and Churchill: 'Portal has everything.'

Oscar Nemon (1906-85), a Yugoslav who had worked in Vienna and Brussels, settled in England before the war. In his youth he modelled Freud and this statue is regarded as his most successful work. His military figures of Portal and Montgomery are regarded as less satisfactory. To avoid distracting visual detail Nemon eliminated all but the slightest details of uniforms. He made several Churchill statues; the last to be erected being a double piece of Sir Winston and Lady Churchill, unveiled in 1991 by Queen Elizabeth the Queen Mother at the Churchills' former country home, Chartwell, Kent, now a National Trust property.

Nearby, with cane under arm and Bible in hand, is **General Charles George Gordon** (1833-85) by Hamo Thornycroft, a statue which once stood in Trafalgar Square. 'Chinese' Gordon was put in command of the 'Ever-Victorious Army' of Chinese troops, officered by Britons and Americans. After 33 engagements it put down the Taiping Rebellion in 1851. When the Mahdi's rebellion broke out in the Sudan Gordon was sent to assist the Egyptian Army. He defended Khartoum for nearly a year. Wolseley was sent to relieve him — but arrived three days too late. Gordon had been killed on 26th January 1885. The government was severely criticised for negligence and Gordon was regarded as a martyr.

The **Royal Air Force Memorial** (1923) fronts the river at Whitehall Stairs. It is by Sir Reginald Blomfield and Sir William Reid Dick, who made the gilt eagle.

In the gardens beyond Horse Guards Avenue is **William Tyndale** (*c*.1484-1536), the reformer and translator of the New Testament, by Sir Joseph Edgar Boehm (1884). After suspicion and persecution in England Tyndale completed his translation in Hamburg and Cologne and began printing there

General Gordon urging his Chinese army into battle, carrying only a cane and revolver, and earning his nickname 'Chinese' Gordon.

Left: *Samuel Plimsoll, 'the seamen's friend', fought against unseaworthy 'coffin ships' and is remembered by the Plimsoll Line on ships and, by association, the sports shoe.*

Right: *Bazalgette gave London the Embankment — 'the finest riverside walk in the world' — and is, appropriately, placed on it.*

in 1525. For a time he was in Henry VIII's favour but the publication of the *Practice of Prelates* in 1530 caused his fall from grace and he was burned as a heretic at Vilvorde in the Netherlands.

Sir Henry Edward Bartle Frere (1815-84), the statesman who stayed in India for 33 years and did invaluable work in the Punjab during the Indian Mutiny and later became Governor of the Cape Colony and High Commissioner of South Africa, has a statue by Sir Thomas Brock (1888).

Another soldier is remembered here: **General Sir James Outram** (1803-63), who went with Havelock to the relief of Lucknow

and was created baronet in 1858. The statue, by Matthew Noble, 1871, shows him wearing the Star of India.

Outside the gardens, by the road and facing the Thames, is the memorial to **Samuel Plimsoll** (1824-98). This is by Ferdinand V. Blundstone, born 1882, who concentrated on public works after winning the Gold Medal and the Landseer and Travelling Scholarships of the Royal Academy. Plimsoll was called 'The Sailors' Friend': he became an MP in 1868 and tackled the problem of the so-called 'coffin ships', old neglected, over-insured and unseaworthy ships sent to sea in the hope of a

Left: *Wilfrid Lawson, the temperance advocate, is neighbour to Robert Burns in Embankment Gardens.*

Right: *The statue of Robert Burns and the Imperial Camel Corps memorial in Embankment Gardens. Burns's statue was the gift of a fellow Scot, John Gordon Crawford. Rossetti said: 'Burns of all poets is the most a man.'*

wreck and an insurance claim. Plimsoll agitated so vehemently that he was suspended from the House of Commons but later the Merchant Shipping Act was passed and the line painted round British ships to prevent overloading is still called the Plimsoll Line. He became first President of the Seamen's and Firemen's Union and the memorial was erected in 1929 by the National Union of Seamen.

At the foot of Northumberland Avenue, near Hungerford Bridge, set into the wall is a bronze mural monument to **Sir Joseph W. Bazalgette**, the creator of the Embankment. An act empowering the Metropolitan Board

of Works to embank the Thames was passed in 1862 and after his superb work Bazalgette was knighted at Windsor in 1874. The dolphin lamp standards and delightful seats with camels and sphinxes date from this time. Look at the **York Water Gate** at the foot of Buckingham Street to see how wide the Thames was before the work was done.

Near Charing Cross Pier is a bronze medallion of **William Schwenck Gilbert** (1836-1911) by Sir George Frampton RA. With Sir Arthur Sullivan (whose own monument is nearby) he produced the immortal operas at the Savoy Theatre near the Strand from 1881: 'His foe was folly and his weapon wit.'

In Victoria Embankment Gardens is a Gloucester newspaper proprietor, Robert Raikes, who started a local Sunday school that was widely copied.

A further section of Embankment Gardens contains a memorial to **Robert Burns** (1759-96), the Scottish poet, whose bronze is by Sir John Steell, 1884. It is not likely that he would have had much in common with his neighbour **Sir Wilfrid Lawson** (1829-1906), the temperance advocate. He was nicknamed 'Dry Wilf' and his monument by David McGill was completed with figures of Temperance, Peace, Fortitude and Charity. They were stolen in 1979. Despite his austere views Lawson had a dry wit. He pointed out that alcohol had raised some £3 million in taxes and that a similar sum had been expended on gunpowder to kill people abroad. 'These sums balance very nicely, *that* is the beauty of the system,' Lawson said.

The memorial to the **Imperial Camel Corps** in the First World War takes the form of a soldier riding a camel and campaign scenes decorate the plinth. The sculptor, Major Cecil Brown, was himself a member of the Camel Corps.

Henry Fawcett (1833-84), the English economist and politician, who was accidentally blinded in a shooting mishap as a young man but rose to be Postmaster General with the innovation of postal orders to his credit, has a bronze medallion and a wall fountain by Mary Grant and Basil Champneys.

Robert Raikes (1735-1811) of Gloucester, the promoter and perhaps the founder of the Sunday School movement, has a monument by Sir Thomas Brock RA, a

Although blind, Fawcett, in Victoria Embankment Gardens, became Postmaster General and introduced postal orders and telegrams.

leading Victorian sculptor with a fashionable practice. Two replicas were made of this statue, which was taken to the sculptor's studio, cleaned and used to make the two bronze castings. One is now in Gloucester and the other in Toronto.

Sir Arthur Seymour Sullivan (1842-1900), who with William Schwenck Gilbert wrote the Savoy operas, has a memorial bust here by Sir William Goscombe John (1903). Sullivan composed *Onward Christian Soldiers* in 1873 and *The Lost Chord*, which was the first phonograph record to be made in England. In 1871 he began an eighteen-year partnership with Gilbert from which came the imperishable Savoy operas including *The Mikado, The Gondoliers* and *The Pirates of Penzance*. A weeping girl embraces the pillar on which Sullivan's bust stands. The inscription is from Colonel Fairfax's song in *The Yeoman of the Guard*:

Is life a boon?
If so it must befall
That death when'er he call
Must call too soon.

The **Savoy Sundial**, erected in 1989, commemorates the Savoy Theatre and the D'Oyly Carte family, who built it.

Near the Savoy, in Embankment Gardens, is this poignant memorial to Sir Arthur Sullivan. His partner, W. S. Gilbert, suggested the inscription, lines from 'The Yeoman of the Guard'.

A monument commemorates **Herbert Francis, 3rd Baron Cheylesmore** (1848-1925), the English soldier, who became Chairman of the London County Council 1912-13. During the First World War he presided over several courts-martial including the one which condemned to death the German spy Karl Loder.

Near here, by the river, is **Cleopatra's Needle**, a pink granite monolith, 68½ feet high and weighing 186 tons, which was erected here in 1878. Mohammed Ali, Viceroy of Egypt, presented it to Britain in 1819 but it was not brought over until many years later, when it was encased in a metal hull and towed to England with great difficulty. Twice it had to be abandoned in storms in the Bay of Biscay and six sailors lost their lives trying to save it. It actually has nothing to do with Cleopatra and was erected at Heliopolis by Thothmes III, a sovereign of the Eighteenth Dynasty, and dedicated to Tum. Companion obelisks stand in New York and Paris. The bronze sphinxes at the base are by G. J. Vulliamy and still bear bomb-scars from the First World War.

On the morning after the unveiling of the column the following note in an unknown

In September 1878 Cleopatra's Needle was set up on Victoria Embankment.

hand was found attached to it:

This monument as some supposes,
Was looked on in old days by Moses,
It passed in time to Greeks and Turks,
And was stuck up here by the Board of
Works.

Opposite the Needle is the **Monument of Belgium's Gratitude for British Aid in 1914-18**, designed by Sir Reginald Blomfield in 1920 with sculptures by Victor Rousseau. Over 250,000 Belgian refugees fled to England in 1914.

At the corner of Savoy Place and Savoy Street, outside the handsome building of the Institute of Electrical Engineers, facing the river stands a modern bronze copy of John Foley's original marble statue, held by the Royal Institution of Great Britain, of **Michael Faraday** (1791-1867), experimental physicist and founder of the science of electro-magnetism. It was erected in 1988. Today the Davy-Faraday Research Laboratory commemorates the two scientists most

closely connected with the Institution's work. A brilliant experimenter, Faraday examined the connections between light, heat, electricity and magnetism and his findings formed the basis of the modern electrical industry. Some, of course, were puzzled by these mysteries. Gladstone is said to have asked Faraday of what use electricity would be. Faraday gave a reassuring answer: 'One day you'll be able to tax it, Sir!'

Notable as the only one in London in which the subject is wearing spectacles is the image of **Sir Walter Besant** (1836-1901), novelist, man of letters, social commentator and historian of London, who, with a dozen others, founded the Society of Authors in 1884 with Alfred, Lord Tennyson, as president. The bronze bust on the Embankment opposite Savoy Street and in the shadow of Waterloo Bridge is a replica of his monument in St Paul's Cathedral. The sculptor was Sir George Frampton (1902). The plaque states: 'Erected by his grateful brethren in literature.'

Beyond Waterloo Bridge, at the corner of Temple Place, is a statue, holding quill pen and dividers, of **Isambard Kingdom Brunel** (1806-59) by Baron Carlo Marochetti (1877). This outstanding engineer assisted his equally famous father, Marc Isambard Brunel, in the construction of the Wapping Tunnel under the Thames, became Chief Engineer to the Great Western Railway in 1833 and later became interested in ship-building. His *Great Western* (1838) was the first steamship to sail the Atlantic regularly; the *Great Britain* (1845) was the world's first large iron steamship, and the first with

The pretty bird-bath in Embankment Gardens near the Temple was a gift of the Temperance Movement to the memory of Lady Henry Somerset.

Michael Faraday, father of the electrical industry, stands in a flower bed outside the Institute of Electrical Engineers by Savoy Street.

FARADAY

a screw propeller. It was used extensively on the Australian run but after some forty years' service was damaged in a storm off Cape Horn and used in the Falkland Islands as a coal hulk. In an epic of towage in 1970 the *Great Britain* was ultimately brought back to Bristol, to the very dock in which she had been built, and was refurbished as a national engineering monument to Brunel's genius. His third ship, the *Great Eastern*, 1858, was the largest ship that had ever been built. She weighed 18,915 tons and could carry 4,000 passengers and enough coal to reach Australia without stopping at coaling ports. But two days before she was due to sail on her first voyage Brunel suffered a severe stroke and died on 7th September 1859.

The gardens to the east of Temple station contain more statues, including **W. E. Forster** (1818-86) by H. R. Pinker. Forster was the statesman and pioneer of mass education who carried through the Elementary Education Bill of 1870.

The figure of a young girl crowns a drinking fountain and bird-bath to the memory of **Lady Henry Somerset**, president of the

National British Women's Temperance
Association. It bears an appropriate motto!

John Stuart Mill (1806-73), the philosopher and economist, is by Thomas
Woolner and the statue was unveiled by his
admirer Professor Fawcett.

On the river parapet facing the gardens
is a memorial by Sir George Frampton to
W. T. Stead (1849-1912), the journalist
and spiritualist, who went down in the
Titanic. He lived at Number 5 Smith
Square, Westminster.

On the 25th anniversary of the accession
of King George V the Port of London Authority, with the king's permission, named
the reach of the Thames between London
Bridge and Westminster Bridge **King's
Reach**. A brass tablet under an imposing
arch records this fact (1935).

Either side of the roadway by Temple
Gardens are two cast-iron **heraldic dragons** of 1849, nostalgic reminders of the
City's Coal Exchange, which was demolished in 1963; they now mark the beginning
of the City of London.

Alongside the dragons, away from the
river, is a plaque commemorating the last
visit of Queen Victoria to the City of London in 1900.

The plaques decorating the memorial on
the Embankment opposite Temple Gardens
to those who were lost at sea in **submarines**
in two world wars are of unusual interest.
One shows the control room of a First World
War submarine with floating ethereal figures; there are lists of submarines lost in
each war, the figures of Truth and Justice
and underneath a depiction of a First World
War submarine on the surface. The design
of 1922 was by F. Brook Hatch and A. H.
Ryan Tenison; additions were made after
the Second War.

The anchors that decorate the surface

*John Stuart Mill's 'On Liberty' warned against
the tyranny of the majority. Though buried in
Avignon, he is commemorated in Embankment
Gardens.*

are in fact brackets on which are hung
wreaths during the service of remembrance
on Armistice Day.

At the river end of Inner Temple Gardens
is a statue of a youth holding a book inscribed with the words of **Charles Lamb,**
the essayist: 'Lawyers, I suppose, were children once!' It is a fibreglass copy by
Margaret Wrightson erected in 1971 of the
original one of 1775 which was set in the
gardens in 1928 and stolen in 1970. Lamb
was born in Crown Office Row and lived in
the Temple until 1817.

Here, too, is a kneeling figure of a **black
with a sundial** on his head. This is said to
be by John Van Nost and to have been
bought in Italy by the Earl of Clare in 1705
and given to Clement's Inn by way of
amends because the Earl's Indian servant
had killed two of the Inn's students. It was
brought here about 1905 and is near Paper
Buildings.

» 14 «
HOLBORN TO ST PAUL'S

From High Holborn turn up Gray's Inn Road and on the left, in the South Square of Gray's Inn (one of the four remaining Inns of Court), is a statue of **Francis Bacon, Baron Verulam and Viscount St Albans** (1561-1626), the treasurer of the Inn, who kept his rooms here from 1576 till his death. He became Lord Chancellor in 1618. The statue is by Frederick W. Pomeroy, a notable sculptor of the later nineteenth century, and it was put up to mark the tercentenary of Bacon's election as treasurer in 1608. The catalpa tree in the garden planted by Bacon is said to have been brought home from America by Sir Walter Raleigh. Bacon was a keen gardener (calling a garden 'the purest of human pleasures') and he laid out the Gray's Inn gardens. They were described by Charles Lamb as 'the best gardens of the Inns of Court, my beloved Temple not forgotten'.

Back in the Holborn roadway, close to Gray's Inn Road, stands the bronze memorial to the **Royal Fusiliers, City of London Regiment** (1922), by Alfred Toft (1862-1949), who was an apprentice at the Wedgwood works and a pupil of Lantéri at the South Kensington Schools.

At the foot of Gray's Inn Road, opposite Staple Inn, are stone obelisks known as the **Holborn Bars** which mark the entrance into the City of London where all but city freemen used to pay tolls when entering with carts.

On the left of Holborn is the fierce red brick Gothic building of the Prudential Assurance Company on the site of Furnival's Inn, where **Charles Dickens** lodged while writing the first part of *Pickwick Papers*. A memorial tablet and bust by Percy Fitzgerald, 1907, recall this fact. *Pickwick Papers* was issued in monthly parts and became an immediate success when the character of Sam Weller was introduced.

Holborn Circus has what has been called the 'most polite statue in London' of **Prince Albert** (1874) by Charles Bacon. Although in uniform, the prince is raising his hat.

At the corner of Cock Lane and Giltspur Street is a fat gilt cherub, **The Golden Boy**, on the corner house, which marks Pie Corner, generally (though some say inaccurately) considered to be the point where the Great Fire of London stopped in 1666. As the fire started in Pudding Lane and finished at Pie Corner, Puritan preachers wasted no time in blaming the catastrophe on London's gluttony! The building was once the inn 'The Fortunes of War', the chief house of call for resurrectionists in the days when body snatchers provided corpses for the surgeons of St Bartholomew's Hospital.

In Giltspur Street is the bust by Sir William Reynolds-Stephens of **Charles Lamb** (1775-1834), the essayist, who was a bluecoat boy for seven years at Christ's Hospital in Newgate Street. 'Perhaps the most beloved name in literature...', the plinth states.

In financial circles it is a rare week that passes without someone quoting 'Gresham's Law' — 'Bad money drives out good money.' It recalls **Sir Thomas**

Left: *Erected in 1923, only five years after the founding of the Royal Air Force by Trenchard, whose statue is close by, the Royal Air Force Memorial overlooks the Thames by the Embankment.*

Right: *In the Victoria Embankment Gardens stands Gordon of Khartoum, holding the cane with which he led his troops against the Taiping rebels.*

Facing page: *Francis Bacon's statue in Gray's Inn marked the tercentenary of his election as treasurer of the Inn.*

Gresham (1519-79), whose statue by H. Bursill (1868) stands on the first floor of Gresham House, next to Holborn Viaduct. Gresham was an astute merchant and financier of the City of London who founded the Royal Exchange and advised four sovereigns, including Elizabeth I, on money matters. He was Elizabeth's 'royal merchant' and was knighted in 1559.

Nearer to St Paul's on the left is the complex of the General Post Office. The King Edward Building has a statue of **Sir Rowland Hill** (1795-1879), who introduced the revolutionary penny postage system in 1840. The statue by Onslow Ford was set up in front of the Royal Exchange and moved here in 1923. The GPO buildings partly shut in the small open space which was once the graveyard of St Botolph Without and is now nicknamed **Postmen's Park**. A cloister wall was put up here in 1880 at the suggestion of G. F. Watts, the sculptor and painter (1817-1904), and over fifty tablets record acts of everyday heroism by policemen, doctors, firemen, labourers and others.

Panyer Alley, near St Paul's, has an old relief of 1688 of a **boy seated on a pannier** or bread basket, recalling that this was once London's bread market and that basket-makers worked nearby. This relief is supposed to mark the highest ground in the City of

London and the inscription reads:
    When ye have sought the City round,
    Yet still is this the highest ground.
The boy is the property of the Vintners' Company and was put in the vaults of the Central Criminal Court during the bombing of the Second World War and was replaced later on Panyer Alley Steps, which lead to Paternoster Square. In fact the record is inaccurate for the land at Cornhill is about one foot higher.

On the wall of St Bartholomew's Hospital (the oldest hospital in London and founded by Rahere in 1123) are memorials to **Sir William Wallace**, who suffered here on 23rd August 1305, and to the **Protestant martyrs** of the reign of Mary I. Seven were burned on 27th June 1558 and the last martyr in England, Bartholomew Legate, died here in 1611. In 1849 during sewer excavations blackened stones, bones and remains of posts and rings were found. On the gateway (which dates from 1702) of St Bartholomew's Hospital is a statue by Francis Bird of **Henry VIII** (1491-1547), who refounded the hospital in 1539.

In founding the penny post Sir Rowland Hill profoundly changed British life. He stands outside the General Post Office in King Edward Street.

» 15 «
ST PAUL'S

Before the west front of the cathedral is a statue of **Queen Anne**, in whose reign the rebuilding of the cathedral after the Great Fire of 1666 was completed. The present statue is a replica of the original by Francis Bird which was erected in 1712. Its placing prompted the following couplet:

Brandy Nan, Brandy Nan, now you're left in the lurch,
Your face to the ginshop, your back to the church.

When the Diamond Jubilee service was to be held at St Paul's in 1897 it was found that Anne's statue seriously blocked the way. It was suggested that the statue be temporarily moved. Queen Victoria was furious and remarked, 'What a ridiculous idea! Move Queen Anne? Most certainly not! Why, it might some day be suggested that *My* statue should be moved and that I should much dislike!'

In the south front pediment is a **phoenix** by Caius Gabriel Cibber which symbolises the rise of the new St Paul's from the old after the Fire. It recalls the incident when Wren asked a workman to bring him a stone at random to mark the centre of the new dome. The man brought a fragment of a tombstone with the word *Resurgam*, meaning 'I shall rise again'.

Francis Bird made the bas-relief of the **Conversion of St Paul** and other figures and decorations on the west and north pediments.

The foundations of the old **St Paul's Cross**, where sermons were preached, her-etics recanted and papal bulls were read, were discovered by the Cathedral Surveyor in 1879 and the site has been clearly defined. Nearby stands the column with St Paul on its top, a memorial to **the Richards family**, cathedral benefactors in the nineteenth century.

The later of the two London statues to **John Wesley** (1703-91), founder of Methodism, stands on the north side of St Paul's Churchyard and was erected by the Aldersgate Trustees of the Methodist Church in 1988. The statue was cast from a marble original made by Samuel Manning and his son in 1839. As a model the Mannings used a bust carved from life by Enoch Wood. The statue shows a man of only 5 feet 1 inch, in canonicals, preaching, prayerbook in hand.

In his 12 foot composition 'Blitz', sculptor John W. Mills commemorates in bronze the 1,002 **firefighters** who died fighting fires in Britain in the Second World War. Another long overdue memorial, 'Blitz' was unveiled on 4th May 1991 by Queen Elizabeth the Queen Mother in Old Change Court, the open space opposite the south side of St Paul's Cathedral. St Paul's itself was saved only by the devoted work of the cathedral staff and the firemen fighting a massive battle in the surrounding streets. The photograph of the cathedral's dome with its gleaming cross silhouetted against the flames and smoke became a world-wide symbol of London's defiance of the German attack.

Near the Barbican, a stone tablet in the

Above: *The statue of Queen Anne by Francis Bird erected in 1712 in front of St Paul's has been replaced by this accurate replica.*

Facing page (left): *Beside St Mary-le-Bow, Cheapside, is John Smith, founder of Jamestown, Virginia, who was once captured by Indians.*

Facing page (right): *This statue of John Wesley is in St Paul's Churchyard.*

CHURCHYARD

By Grace ye are saved through Faith

John Wesley

Father of Methodism

1703 — 1791

wall of Fore Street, round the corner from Wood Street which crosses London Wall, records: 'On this site at 12.15 a.m. on 25th August 1940, fell **the first bomb** in the City of London in the Second World War.'

Hearing Henry II's angry words 'Will no one rid me of this turbulent priest?' and taking him at his word, four of Henry's knights murdered **Thomas à Becket**, Archbishop of Canterbury, at the high altar of Canterbury Cathedral. It had been a stormy relationship. Henry, a proud, wilful man, realised that to avoid offending the papacy he needed an ally in the post of Archbishop of Canterbury and, in 1162, appointed his Chancellor, Thomas à Becket, to the post, against Becket's will. Arguments intensified, Becket fled to France and returned for

The Firefighters' Memorial, 'Blitz', unveiled in 1991.

a brief reconciliation with the king. Finally the fateful words were uttered and on 29th December 1170 the deed was done. E. Bainbridge Copnall, sculptor of Becket's bronze statue on the south side of St Paul's Churchyard (1973), shows the archbishop fallen and at the point of death. The siting is appropriate as Becket was born in nearby Cheapside, immediately east of St Paul's and where the next statue is located.

A seafarer, adventurer and member of an expedition to Virginia in 1607, **Captain John Smith** (1580-1631) became 'First among the Leaders of the Settlement of Jamestown, Virginia, from which began the overseas expansion of the English Speaking Peoples'. A romantic story is told of his rescue from death by crushing by the eleven-year-old Princess Pocahontas after Smith was captured by the Powhatan Indians. Smith was elected the colony's 'Governor' in 1608. He returned to England in 1609-10, where he worked energetically to promote more expeditions, and mapped the North American coast from Nova Scotia to Rhode Island. As Admiral of New England he advised the Pilgrim Fathers but because of a clash of personalities did not sail with them. He continued to write and publish widely: his work is of great historical value.

Smith's statue, which was unveiled by Queen Elizabeth the Queen Mother on 31st October 1960, is a replica by Charles Rennick of one in Virginia by William Couper. It stands in the old churchyard beside St Mary-le-Bow, Cheapside, and was presented by the Jamestown Foundation of the Commonwealth of Virginia to commemorate Smith's return to England. He appears in Elizabethan dress with a book in his right hand and a sword in his left — a good combination for an enterprising pioneer.

» 16 «
BANK OF ENGLAND, ROYAL EXCHANGE

Around the Bank of England are sculptures by Sir Charles Wheeler including, on the pediment, the **Old Lady of Threadneedle Street** with a model of the old Bank on her knee and a pile of coins at her side. The present building was built by Sir Herbert Baker in 1925-39, within Soane's original walls.

Sir John Soane, the architect to the Bank from 1788 to 1833, has his statue by Sir William Reid Dick at the north side at the corner of Lothbury.

Sir Henry Cheere's statue of **William III**, commissioned by the Bank's directors in 1734 in gratitude to their patron, now stands in the Bank of England Museum.

Above the Corinthian portico of the Royal Exchange is a group representing **Commerce** holding the charter of the Exchange, attended by the Lord Mayor, British merchants and various foreign citizens.

The 177 foot high campanile with bells has a statue of **Sir Thomas Gresham** (1519-79), founder of the Exchange, and an 11 foot long grasshopper (his crest) as a weathervane, recalling the old story that as a baby Gresham was lost in a field and was found through the chirping of grasshoppers. The sculptures are by Westmacott and the statue by William Behnes (1845).

In front of the Exchange is an equestrian statue of the **Duke of Wellington**, one of the chief works of Sir Francis Legatt Chantrey, which shows the Duke riding without stirrups. It was unveiled in the Duke's presence and the story is that, the ceremony over, the Duke approached the great door (normally sacrosanct to members only) to enter the Exchange. The doorkeeper tactfully allowed him to enter without argument while the band played *See the Conquering Hero Comes.*

Also before the Exchange is the **War Memorial to London Troops** (1920) by Sir Aston Webb and Alfred Drury (who made the figures).

Behind the Exchange was a seated figure of **George Peabody** (1795-1869), the American philanthropist responsible for many housing projects for the working people of London. The first Peabody Buildings were opened in Spitalfields in 1864. The statue, by W. S. Story, was unveiled on 23rd July 1869 by the Prince of Wales. It has been removed and its future is uncertain.

Still here is the bust of **Paul Julius Reuter** (1819-99), who founded the world news organisation that bears his name in Number 1 Royal Exchange Buildings on 14th October 1851. It is by Michael Black.

On the north side is a statue by Joseph (1845) of **Hugh Myddleton**, whose scheme brought fresh water from Hertfordshire springs to London. (See chapter 17 for a fuller account of this project.) Also on the north side is a statue by Carew of **Richard Whittington** (died 1423), Lord Mayor of London three times as Bow bells foretold.

The equestrian statue of the Duke of Wellington by Chantrey stands outside the Royal Exchange.

» 17 «
BANK TO ISLINGTON, BISHOPSGATE

On the wall of the Northampton Polytechnic, Finsbury, is a bronze medallion of the bearded **William George Spencer Scott Compton, 5th Marquis of Northampton**, put up by his London tenants. The Marquis, born in 1851, was MP for Warwickshire and Barnsley and held the extraordinary post of Special Envoy to the Courts of France, Italy, Greece and Turkey to announce the accession of George V in 1910.

Overlooking the forecourt of Liverpool Street station, look below the war memorial of the Great Eastern Railway to see the bronze medallion to **Captain Charles Algernon Fryatt** (1872-1916), master of the railway mail steamer *Brussels*, who was shot at Bruges by the Germans in 1916. On 28th March 1915, when bringing the *Brussels* from Parkstone to Rotterdam he was met by the German submarine U33 near the Maas lightship. He disregarded the signal to stop and steered for the submarine, which escaped by diving. Later the Germans asserted that he had allowed the U33 to approach to spy on her and on the night of 23rd June, while steaming for home, the *Brussels* was captured by a torpedo-boat flotilla and taken to Zeebrugge. Fryatt was tried and shot the same day.

Field Marshal Sir Henry Wilson, Bart (1864-1922), was part of the tragedy. He unveiled the Fryatt memorial but died within two hours of doing so, shot on the doorstep of his home by two Irish terrorists. His grave, next to Wellington's in St Paul's, states unequivocally 'Murdered outside his home, 36 Eaton Place, June 22, 1922'. It was Wilson who was responsible for the high state of preparation of the British Expeditionary Force in 1914. Later he was elected to Parliament as Conservative member for North Down in Northern Ireland and in some way this must have led to the murder.

The older of **John Wesley's** statues — it cost £1,000 contributed by Methodist children — was erected at the City Road Chapel at the centenary of Wesley's death. It is the work of J. Adams Acton, 'the Methodist sculptor', and was unveiled by Dr W. F. Moulton, president of the Wesleyan Conference. (Moulton's own bust, also by Acton, is inside the chapel.) Wesley's words 'The world is my parish' are on the plinth.

At Oxford Wesley (1703-91) joined his brother Charles in a 'Holy Club', from which Methodism — life conducted by 'rule and method' — evolved. Wesley aimed at recalling the Church of England to its spiritual mission and opened the first Methodist chapel in Bristol in 1739. His evangelical style attracted crowds of labourers, miners, shopkeepers and the lower middle classes and in April 1777 the City Road Chapel (the 'cathedral of Methodism') was built, with a house for Wesley next door. George III took an interest and provided masts from the royal dockyard for the chapel gallery. They are still to be seen as well as Wesley's pulpit. Wesley preached widely until late in his life; he is said to have travelled 250,000 miles on horseback and to have given 40,000 sermons. He died in his house in March 1791 and is buried in the chapel graveyard.

Wesley wielded much influence and had admirers in many walks of society. But as time passed some, who at first approved, came to dislike aspects of Methodism such as the 'love-feasts', the fainting-fits, tears and groans induced by Wesley's preaching style and what one observer termed 'moral smugness'. At the end of his life, for example, Wesley confessed that in fifty years he had wasted fifteen minutes reading a worthless book.

When crowds were great Wesley preached out of doors in **Bunhill Fields**, from 1685 to 1852 the principal nonconformist burial ground. The name derives from 'bonehill' for it was here in 1547 that Protector Somerset dumped the contents of the St Paul's charnel-house. At the second turning to the south from the main walk is the grave-effigy of **John Bunyan** by E. C. Papworth, 1862, restored 1950.

On Islington Green is a statue of **Sir Hugh Myddleton** (*c.*1560-1631), who in 1606 made an offer to Parliament to bring a supply of pure drinking water (of which there was a great shortage) to London. At this time water was still brought round by horse and cart with resultant disease and inconvenience. The New River Company's supply was piped 38^3/$_4$ miles from the springs of the Lea Valley, Hertfordshire, to the New River Head, where reservoirs still stand. Myddleton's work, which took four years to complete and from which grew the Metropolitan Water Board, was a feat of its time. The present offices of the Board incorporate a room with fine plasterwork and panelling from the Water House of 1693. The names of the streets about, Chadwell Street, Amwell Street (named after the springs from which the water came), River Street and Myddleton Square, recall the work. The statue, by John Thomas, was unveiled by Gladstone in 1862.

The statue of Sir Hugh Myddleton (right) and (below) John Thomas, the sculptor.

» 18 «

THE CITY TO THE SOUTH AND EAST OF THE BANK, TOWER HILL

After many years in the outer wall of St Swithin's church the **London Stone** is now in the wall of the new office buildings opposite Cannon Street station. This is generally believed to be the *milliarium* of Roman London from which road distances were measured. In Shakespeare's *Henry VI* Jack Cade the rebel struck his sword on this stone exclaiming, 'Now is Mortimer Lord of this city'. St Swithin's was demolished in 1962 after bomb damage.

A particularly attractive example of painted Coade stone survives on a corbel on the west wall of the Vintners' Company in Vintners Place off Upper Thames Street by Southwark Bridge. It is the **Vintry Schoolboy**, a child of the Vintry Ward School of 1840; he is in its uniform of long trousers, frock coat, bands and bow tie. As his badge shows, his school number was 30. The Vintry Ward was the site occupied by the vintners from Bordeaux who anciently settled on the bank of the Thames and landed their wines here.

James Hulbert (died 1720), Prime Warden of the Fishmongers' Company (1718-20), is remembered by a marble statue by

James Hulbert, Prime Warden of the Fishmongers' Company, is glimpsed from the river walk by London Bridge, in the courtyard of the Fishmongers' Hall.

Robert Easton which was moved to this site in 1978 and stands in the courtyard of Fishmongers' Hall, opening on to the river walkway by London Bridge. (It is reached from Swan Lane off Lower Thames Street.) When Hulbert made his will he planned an almshouse for twenty poor persons but, like Thomas Guy (chapter 20), his investment in South Sea stock was sold at exactly the right moment. The Court of Fishmongers found itself in command of £9,467 2s 5d (about £250,000 in modern terms), enough to accommodate forty persons rather than the expected twenty. £2,000 secured the building; the rest of the investments provided benefits: residents were warm and dry, with a stuff gown, a chauldron (32 bushels) of coals each year, 3 shillings a week and a Christmas bonus, an annual visit from the Wardens and services in their own chapel. They doubtless felt — and rightly — that fate had been very kind to them.

Leading north from London Bridge is King William Street, named after William IV. To the east of this is the **Monument** to the Great Fire of London, 1666

In his Seething Lane garden Pepys buried his Parmesan cheese during the Great Fire. His bust was erected on the site of his garden in 1983.

On Tower Hill is the site where Thomas More and many other prisoners from the Tower were executed. Behind is the Merchant Seamen's War Memorial, to which a sunken garden was added after the Second World War.

— a fluted Doric column, 202 feet high and exactly 202 feet from the point in Pudding Lane where the fire started. This was erected to Christopher Wren's designs in 1671-7. A winding staircase of 311 steps leads to the top platform, from which there is a magnificent view over London. Originally it was intended to place a statue of Charles II on top but this proved too expensive and a flaming gilt urn finial, 42 feet high, was substituted. The bas-reliefs are the work of Caius Gabriel Cibber and amongst the figures is London being raised by Father Time, while on the east side is a list of Lord Mayors during the period of erection and on the north an account of the fire. To the north of the Monument is Eastcheap, which leads east towards Tower Hill. At Trinity Square, Muscovy Street leads into Seething Lane.

In the garden of his Seething Lane house, **Samuel Pepys**, naval administrator and diarist (1633-1703), dug a hole when the Great Fire of London threatened and hid certain state papers — and his precious Parmesan cheese. Pepys, long an absentee from the statue scene, now has a bronze bust by Karin Jonzen (1983) in Seething Lane Gardens, on the site of his old home.

Samuel had luck in his patron and first cousin Edward Montagu, a Cromwellian statesman and admiral. In the republican administration set up after Cromwell's death Montagu developed Royalist sympathies and, after the Restoration, rose, taking Pepys with him as Clerk of the Acts to the Navy Board, responsible for the civil administration of the Navy. The Clerk's official lodgings were in Seething Lane. It was from here that Pepys watched the spread of the Great Fire. It began on Saturday 2nd September 1666. At first no one appreciated the danger: Pepys himself looked out and went back to bed. But later he alerted

Charles II, who personally organised firefighting among the panic-stricken population. Houses were blown up to create firebreaks and thatch was pulled from roofs. But not until the following Wednesday did rain and quieter weather make real control possible. The fire swept the city from the Tower to Fleet Street; 400 streets, 13,200 houses and many landmarks had vanished. St Paul's was a ruin.

From 1660 to 1669, when he feared his eyesight was failing, Samuel Pepys kept his famous diary, which remains an unexcelled picture of contemporary life, revealing Samuel's own lovable character. In 1673 he was appointed first Secretary to the Admiralty. Now one of the leading civil servants in the country, by 1678 he had turned the Navy into a powerful disciplined force, become an MP and spokesman for the service he had created. But in the confused politics of the time he was accused of involvement in the Popish Plot and was imprisoned for six weeks in the Tower, although charges were dropped. He was then out of office for five years until Charles II, anxious about naval efficiency, made him Secretary for Admiralty Affairs, a post he retained under James II. When James was dethroned Pepys was again falsely accused of treason and Jacobitism. He resigned, retired to private life and died at Clapham on 26th May 1703.

Back at Trinity Square on Tower Hill is a small paved area with chains round it which marks the **site of the scaffold** where many prisoners in the Tower met their deaths from 1388 to 1747. As a rule those of royal blood were executed within the Tower and those of common blood outside. Lord Lovat was the last to be executed here in 1747 for his part in the Rebellion of 1745 and had his final revenge (and was, it is said, amused) by the sight of a stand containing a thousand of his Whig enemies collapsing under their weight. Others executed here included Sir Thomas More, Archbishop Laud and the Earl of Surrey.

Also in the garden of Trinity Square is the impressive **Merchant Seamen's War Memorial** to men of the Merchant Navy, fishing fleets and lighthouse and pilotage services who died in the two world wars. A colonnade commemorates the First World War and a sunken garden designed by Sir Edward Maufe (with sculptures by Sir Charles Wheeler) commemorating the Second World War was opened in 1955.

Trinity House on the north side of the Square has the duty of erecting and maintaining lighthouses, lightships and other sea marks and it is the principal pilotage authority in Britain. The building was rebuilt in 1793-5 for the 'Guild, Fraternity and Brotherhood of the Trinity, most Glorious and Undivided' and on the façade are the arms of the corporation and medallions of **George III and Queen Charlotte**, king and queen at the time of building.

The late eighteenth-century Italian bronze statue of the Roman emperor **Trajan** (AD 53 to 117) stands bareheaded, in the short tunic of the Roman general, in Trinity Place by Tower Hill station, backed by the longest surviving section of the original London Wall. It has no real connection with the neighbourhood except through the Reverend P. B. 'Tubby' Clayton MC, joint

The Roman emperor Trajan, an Italian copy erected here in 1980, stands by Tower Hill.

founder of TOC H with the Reverend Nevill Talbot. Clayton, vicar of All Hallows church nearby, found the statue in a Southampton scrapyard. It was presented to the Tower Hill Improvement Trust and erected here in 1980.

All Hallows is the guild church of the world-wide TOC H movement which was founded to perpetuate the Christian fellowship of the Talbot Houses at Poperinghe and Ypres in Belgium, which provided places of rest and recreation for troops temporarily withdrawn from the front in the First World War. (TOC H is 'T H' in the old Army signallers' alphabet.) The name Talbot commemorates Lieutenant Gilbert Talbot, killed in action in 1915. All Hallows escaped the Great Fire of 1666 by the swift action of Admiral Sir William Penn, who ordered sailors working nearby to blow up houses between the fire and the church. He had a special interest; his son William — Penn of Pennsylvania — had been baptised at All Hallows on 23rd October 1644.

Today the ivory trade has ceased but in the nineteenth century ivory was widely used for articles from paper knives to piano keys. Ivory House, in St Katherine Dock east of Tower Bridge, built by Aitcheson (1854), stored ivory upstairs and port in the cellars. These days are recalled by the **Ivory House Gates** in East Smithfield, the one-way street behind the old Royal Mint, with a handsome pair of fibreglass elephants designed by Peter Drew (1973).

» 19 «
EAST END AND DOCKLANDS

In Kingsland Road, Shoreditch, over the door of the Geffrye Museum, is a statue made for the Ironmongers' Company by John Nost (1723) of **Sir Robert Geffrye** (1613-1704), Master of the Company and Lord Mayor of London, 1685-6. In his will, Geffrye, who lost heavily in the Great Fire but recovered his fortune, left money for the establishment of almshouses and a chapel. The statue is a replica of the original which accompanied the almshouses when they moved out of London. The buildings became the Geffrye Museum.

In Whitechapel Road, opposite the London Hospital, is a memorial to **Edward VII** (1841-1910) erected by the Jews of East London. His medallion portrait is flanked by Justice and Liberty, with cherubs holding a book, a steamer and a motor car. The sculptor was W. S. Frith. The column was erected in 1911 by local Jews who felt that Edward's support had helped their case for admission after the Russian persecution.

In the courtyard garden of the London Hospital is a huge bronze statue of Edward's **Queen Alexandra** (1844-1925). Alexandra was a tireless supporter of London hospitals. The inscription notes that in 1900 she 'introduced to England the Finsen light cure for Lupus and presented the first lamp to this hospital'. The statue, by George Edward Wade, shows her in coronation robes with crown and sceptre. It was erected in 1908.

Whitechapel Road continues east to become Mile End Road. **William Booth's** open-air services in 1868, on the piece of ground called Mile End Waste, were the start of the Salvation Army. At the beginning of the Mile End Road is a bronze bust by George Edward Wade of Booth (1829-1912) which was added in 1929 to a commemorative stone laid in 1910 by Commissioner Rees. In 1979 a fibreglass replica of Booth's statue at the Salvation Army's Training College was erected, painted grey and filled with concrete to deter vandals. Nevertheless they quickly damaged it and the statue was removed.

Mile End Road continues east to become Bow Road, where outside Bow churchyard is another bronze statue to **William Ewart Gladstone**, one of that rare breed of statue set up during its subject's lifetime. It was sculpted by Albert Bruce-Joy (1882) and was the gift of Theodore Bryant, a prominent Liberal and member of the match manufacturing company, whose works was nearby. Its erection marked Gladstone's completion of fifty years as an MP.

In a time of great changes the **Navigators**, in painted ceramic tiles by the river frontage, seems to be safe in the King Edward VII Memorial Park, laid out on the site of the old Shadwell Fish Market in 1922. (Part of the park is over the Rotherhithe Tunnel.) From here in 1553 a number of ships set sail under **Sir Hugh Willoughby** to seek the North-west Passage to India, unsuccessfully. In 1576 **Sir Martin Frobisher** sailed; he too failed, although he made two further attempts, and had Frobisher Bay in northern Canada

named after him.   Also remembered are **Stephen and William Borough** and other sixteenth-century navigators and their crews who set out from here.   The park has a medallion monument to **Edward VII**, by Sir Bertram Mackennal RA, unveiled by George V in 1922.

THIS TABLET IS IN MEMORY OF
SIR HUGH WILLOUGHBY, STEPHEN BOROUGH,
WILLIAM BOROUGH, SIR MARTIN FROBISHER
AND OTHER NAVIGATORS WHO, IN THE LATTER
HALF OF THE SIXTEENTH CENTURY, SET SAIL
FROM THIS REACH OF THE RIVER THAMES NEAR
RATCLIFF CROSS
TO EXPLORE THE NORTHERN SEAS.

ERECTED BY THE LONDON COUNTY COUNCIL, 1922

Above left: *A car of 1911 and a boat are unusual accessories for 'Liberty' on Edward VII's monument in Mile End Road.*

Above right: *The Navigators' Memorial was set up in the Edward VII Memorial Park in 1922.*

Below left: *On the Mile End Road, William Booth's tunic bears the Salvation Army badge and motto 'Blood and Fire'.*

Below right: *This medallion portrait of Edward VII is on the commemorative pillar in the Edward VII Memorial Park.*

The statue of Labour Prime Minister Clement Attlee is outside Limehouse Library.

On 30th November 1988 a former Labour Prime Minister, Lord Wilson of Rievaulx, unveiled a statue outside Limehouse public library of **Clement Richard Attlee** (1883-1967), Britain's first post-war Labour Prime Minister. Attlee had been Deputy Prime Minister in Churchill's wartime coalition cabinet, then led the Labour Party to a landslide victory in the 1945 General Election. He was a former Mayor of Stepney and had been MP for Limehouse. His post-war government proceeded with a programme of nationalisation including the railways, the mines, the steel industry and utilities, established the National Health Service, carried through educational reforms and granted independence to India and Pakistan. Attlee's statue portrays him speaking, with a bundle of papers in his right hand and his left characteristically holding his left lapel.

Vast crowds attended the funeral at Trinity Chapel, Poplar, of **Richard Green** (1806-63), shipowner and philanthropist, far more than could be accommodated in the church. So great was his popularity that all the surrounding streets were packed and all the ships in the Thames, not only his own, showed the conventional maritime marks of respect. 'I had no time to hesitate,' was Green's favourite saying. It typified a man noted for clear thought, quick decisions and business acumen, who devoted much of his life to the improvement of the lot of the merchant seaman. Contributions towards his statue came from all over the world. It was unveiled in East India Dock Road a mere three years after his death. The sculptor was E. W. Wyon and Green is shown seated, his Newfoundland dog 'Hector' sitting beside him.

At the entrance to the East India Dock (closed in 1967) is the **Virginia Settlers' Memorial**, unveiled here in 1951 and recast in 1970, commemorating the sailing in 1606 of three small ships, the *Susan Constant*, *Godspeed* and *Discovery* (a mere 20 tons), with the first permanent colonists for Jamestown, Virginia. They included Captain John Smith, whose energy and resource were vital in the infant colony. The tablet, at Brunswick Wharf, was presented by the people of Virginia in 1928. It lies within the boundaries of Blackwall Power Station, which is due for demolition, but in the past permission to visit the memorial has sometimes been granted.

Above: *The statues fronting the north wing terrace of St Thomas's Hospital: (from left to right) Edward VI (1681); Edward VI (1737); Sir Robert Clayton, by Grinling Gibbons; Florence Nightingale ('the Lady of the Lamp'), who cared for 10,000 soldiers at Scutari Hospital.*

Below left: *Lord Nuffield is reputed to have given £57 million to charities. Guy's Hospital was a beneficiary and Nuffield's statue stands here.*

Below right: *Thomas Guy's statue is in the forecourt of the hospital he founded.*

» 20 «
SOUTH BANK AND SURREY SIDE

Once the grounds of the notorious Bethlem Hospital (which now houses the Imperial War Museum), the Geraldine Mary Harmsworth Park was created in 1926 by Lord Rothermere, younger brother of Viscount Northcliffe, in memory of his mother. In the north angle of the park is an obelisk erected in 1771 in St George's Circus nearby in honour of **Brass Crosby** (1725-93), a magistrate and Lord Mayor of London who was sent to the Tower in 1771 for stoutly refusing to convict the printer who published reports of proceedings in Parliament.

Lambeth Palace, by the Thames at Lambeth Bridge, is the seat of the Archbishops of Canterbury and has a memorial cross by Sir William Reynolds Stephens (born 1862) to **Randall Thomas, Lord Davidson** (1848-1930), Archbishop of Canterbury for 25 years. It stands in a courtyard at the Palace. Lord Davidson was the 96th Archbishop of Canterbury and of a reforming turn of mind: the rejection of his 1928 prayerbook measure was a bitter personal blow. After his resignation the king bestowed a barony on him, an almost unique honour for a churchman.

The Albert Embankment leads north alongside the Thames, from Lambeth Palace to St Thomas's Hospital, which has four statues fronting the north wing terrace overlooking the garden, placed there in 1976. **King Edward VI** (1537-53), refounder of St Thomas's after its closure by Henry VIII, the central stone figure of the old hospital gateway, sculpted in 1682 by Thomas

Cartwright, the hospital mason, following plans of Nathaniel Hanwell, appears here, together with a second statue of the king in bronze erected in 1737, by Peter Scheemakers. Edward VI was deeply concerned about the welfare of the poor and sick, proposed a scheme for Bridewell Hospital and made over funds to the royal hospitals.

Another benefactor to be found here is **Sir Robert Clayton** (1629-1707), a wealthy broker and scrivener. Left a fortune by his uncle, he became Lord Mayor of London in 1679 and was MP for the City of London 1678-81 and President of St Thomas's. His statue, one of only two outdoor sculptures in London by Grinling Gibbons, first erected in 1702, was moved to this site in 1976.

Finally, and inevitably since the Nightingale School of Nursing has been at St Thomas's since 1860, a copy of Walker's statue of **Florence Nightingale** (1820-1910) was erected in 1958 but disappeared. A further version was placed here in 1976. The lamp in both this and the Waterloo Place statues is of Roman design and not like the lamp Miss Nightingale used at Scutari.

Across Westminster Bridge from St Thomas's is the **Coade Stone Lion** (1837), formerly the trademark of the Lion Brewery on the South Bank, demolished in 1948 to make room for the Royal Festival Hall. The lion was designed by W. F. Woodington: the Coade family always used artists of the highest quality for their designs. One of the lion's paws is inscribed 'W. F. W. Coade 24 May 1837'. The story is told that when Emile Zola was staying at the Savoy Hotel, immediately across the river from the brewery, he saw the lion early one morning, apparently rising through the morning mist on the water. He

The lion, of Coade stone, moved upstream to Westminster Bridge from the South Bank Brewery.

called delightedly to his wife: 'Come and see, here's the British lion waiting to bid us goodday!' The lion, which formed part of the decorations for the Festival of Britain (1951), was moved to this site in 1966. Coade stone, a kind of terracotta much used for the decoration of London buildings in the late eighteenth and early nineteenth centuries, was impervious to water and was by far the most durable artificial stone ever made. When the factory closed in 1840 the secret of its manufacture was lost.

The lion is by County Hall, to the north of which is a memorial by Ian Walters to over 2,100 volunteers who went to Spain and fought in the **International Brigade** against fascism (1936-9).

Further north along the riverside walk, between the Hungerford railway bridge and the Royal Festival Hall, is a colossal bust by Ian Walters (1985) of **Nelson Mandela**, deputy president

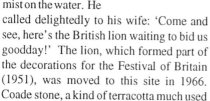

Ian Walters sculpted this bust of Nelson Mandela which now stands on the west side of the Royal Festival Hall.

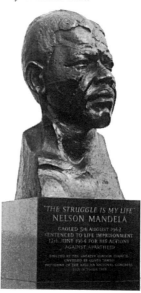

of the African National Congress (ANC). He was released in February 1990 after a long period of imprisonment in South Africa.

At the corner of Park Street and Bankside is a tablet marking the approximate site of the Elizabethan **Globe Theatre**, erected by Richard and Cuthbert Burbage about 1598, where Shakespeare acted with the King's Company until 1612. The tablet was unveiled in 1909 by Sir Herbert Beerbohm Tree, the actor-manager.

In the courtyard of Guy's Hospital at London Bridge is a statue of **Thomas Guy** (1645-1724), the bookseller who made money by selling bibles and by speculation (some say in South Sea stock) and built up a fortune of £200,000 which he used to endow the hospital in 1722. An old story tells that Guy contemplated marriage with his maidservant Sally, of whose frugal ways he approved. The engagement was announced and pre-wedding house repairs set in train, with Sally supervising the workmen. Unfortunately she ordered the repair of the footpath outside the neighbour's house as well as that in front of Guy's house. 'On the mistress's orders,' Guy was told by the workmen and was so alarmed at these signs of dangerous extravagance that he cancelled all arrangements — and gave his money to the hospital. He is buried in the hospital chapel. The statue is by Scheemakers and the subjects on the pedestal are the same as those used by Hogarth on the staircase of St Bartholomew's Hospital: the Good Samaritan and the Pool of Bethesda.

Also here is one of the alcoves from old London Bridge, demolished in 1830. In another courtyard is a statue of **William Richard Morris, 1st Viscount Nuffield** (1877-1963), the car manufacturer and philanthropist who made generous gifts to Guy's Hospital. Lord Nuffield began work as a cycle repairer in a shed at Cowley, Oxford, turned to car making and built up a fortune: by 1938 he had given £11,500,000 for research, education and charity but still kept

to his modest, unaffected way of life. The Nuffield Foundation was founded in 1943 with an endowment of £10,000,000 — one of the largest charitable trusts ever conceived, with an annual income of £400,000. In all by 1957 he had given away £57,000,000.

South of Guy's Hospital, Borough High Street leads to Trinity Street and Trinity Church Square, which can perhaps claim possession of London's oldest statue. It was brought here from the old Palace of Westminster in 1822 and probably dates from about 1395. Although this is not entirely certain it appears to be of **Alfred the Great** and it is in any case a strong claimant for seniority together with the statue of Elizabeth I at St Dunstan-in-the-West. Trinity Square was laid out in 1824 when the statue was erected.

Further south, leading east from Elephant

Possibly the oldest outdoor statue in London is in Trinity Church Square ; it may be of Alfred the Great.

and Castle, the New Kent Road has a memorial garden to Dickens's famous character **David Copperfield**, with a stone statue of a cherub blowing into a conch shell. Dickens wrote: 'I came to a stop in the Kent Road at a terrace with a piece of water before it and a great foolish image in the middle blowing on a dry shell.' The water has now gone. A memorial was set up here in 1932 by the Dickens Fellowship.

Back by the river, Tooley Street runs from London Bridge to Tower Bridge Road. Here, by the south end of Tower Bridge, is **Colonel Samuel Bourne Bevington** (1832-1917), who ran a family leather business in

Samuel Bourne Bevington, popular first Mayor of Bermondsey, stands at the junction of Tooley Street and Tower Bridge Road.

Ernest Bevin, Foreign Secretary in the postwar Labour government. His bust is at the southern end of Tower Bridge.

Bermondsey and was an important employer and popular man in the borough. In 1900 he was Bermondsey's first mayor, and the local leader of many projects for social reform, especially education. He was also a colonel in the Volunteers. His bronze statue, in his mayoral robes, is by Sydney Marsh (1910).

Next to the Bevington statue is a bust of **Ernest Bevin** (1881-1951), who, although of humble beginnings and self-educated, rose to be one of the most impressive and admired Foreign Secretaries of the twentieth century. He created the Transport and General Workers' Union and later was chairman of the Trades Union Congress and Minister of Labour in the War Cabinet. His bronze bust, by E. Whitney Smith, was erected in 1955. As Bevin is particularly remembered as a champion of the dockers, it is inscribed 'The Dockers' KC'.

These streets once echoed to the sound of horses' hooves; costers' carts, brewers' drays, milk floats, work horses of all kinds were to be seen. They have their memorial in **the Circle Dray Horse**, a full-sized bronze dray horse on a plinth in the centre of a new residential development in Queen Elizabeth Street between the Thames and Tooley Street. It commemorates the Courage Dray Horse Stables which stood on this site. The horse was flown in over London by helicopter when it was placed in position in October 1987.

From Tower Bridge Road, the Old Kent Road leads south-east to New Cross. At New Cross Gate, Pepys Road goes south to Haberdashers' Aske's School, in front of which stands a statue of **Robert Aske**.

Aske was apprenticed to a haberdasher and East India merchant dealing in silk. In 1666 he became an alderman of the City of London and in 1685 Master of his livery. His will gave money to establish almshouses for poor freemen of the company and to educate twenty boys.

Aske's statue shows him in his livery robes; at his side is a scroll with the school's motto 'Serve and obey'; he holds another scroll bearing plans of the original almshouses and school. The statue is made of Coade stone and is by William Croggan, a director of the Coade works.

From New Cross Gate, New Cross Road runs to Greenwich, location of three fine statues.

General James Wolfe (1727-59) lived at Macartney House. His statue, presented by the Canadian people, is by Dr Tait Mackenzie (1930) and stands on a terrace adjoining the former Observatory. The general gazes across London from the heights of the park. Curiously like Nelson, with a character combining verve and prudence, and a strict but humane officer, Wolfe is remembered for his capture of Quebec at the battle of the

Plains of Abraham in 1759. The statue was unveiled by the Marquis de Montcalm, a descendant of Wolfe's adversary at the battle. After Wolfe's death a prize was offered for the best epitaph to him. A very mixed group of poets entered and one feels that the less inspired efforts should never have seen the light of day. One, sent to the *Public Ledger*, ran:

He march'd without dread or fears
At the head of his bold grenadiers
And what was more remarkable — nay
    very particular
He climbed up rocks that were perpendicular!

Wolfe's statue in Greenwich was unveiled by a descendant of his French opponent, Montcalm.

Wolfe himself had better taste in poetry for on the eve of the battle he repeated nearly the whole of Gray's *Elegy,* remarking that he would rather have written that poem than beat the French on the following day. Yet, at the end, his military instincts were again to the fore for his last recorded words were: 'What, do they run already? Then I die happy.'

The granite statue of **William IV** (1765-1837), the 'Sailor King', in King William Walk in Greenwich Park, came from King William Street in the City. It is by Samuel Nixon and shows the king in the uniform of Lord High Admiral with the Garter. William entered the Navy in 1779 and saw service in America and the West Indies; later he became Lord High Admiral. His unassumingly correct private life was much admired. (A veil was drawn over the twenty years when he had lived with Mrs Jordan, the actress, who bore him ten children.) In agreeable contrast to George IV, he hated pomp and ceremony. In a period of popular democracy he was the only European monarch to survive: while other countries in Europe were in turmoil Britain went steadily forward, passing the Reform Bill in 1832, abolishing slavery in the colonies in 1833, reforming the Poor Laws in 1834 and municipal legislation in 1835, led by a man who, in his youth, had been best man to Captain Horatio Nelson.

Marble captured from a French ship in the Mediterranean ended as a statue of **George II** (1683-1760) by J. M. Rysbrack, which stands between the Royal Naval College buildings at Greenwich and the river. He appears in Roman dress, inappropriately, since he, like his father before him, was a predominantly German prince. Notable events of his reign were the 1745 Rebellion, the Capture of Quebec from the French

in 1759, the French defeat in India, the rise of Methodism and a golden period of letters, of Sterne, Smollett, Goldsmith and Johnson. George II achieved some personal distinction by being the last British monarch to lead his troops into battle, at Dettingen in 1743.

Until it was burned down in 1936 **Sir Joseph Paxton's** glass masterpiece, the Crystal Palace, was a landmark visible from every part of London. Paxton (1801-65), head gardener to the Duke of Devonshire at Chatsworth, was both gardener and architect with creative building skills, noted for his huge glass conservatories. In 1850 when 233 other plans for the Great Exhibition had been rejected, Paxton prepared blueprints in a mere nine days, submitted them and was successful. The building was erected in Hyde Park in 1851 to acclaim, Paxton was knighted and in 1853 superintended the equally daunting task of dismantling and re-erecting the 'Crystal Palace' in Sydenham. Paxton was a man of surpassing energy; all this time he was still superintending the Chatsworth garden and in addition became Liberal MP for Coventry, a seat he held until his death. He is remembered in the Crystal Palace grounds by a huge bust, five times life size, on a red brick plinth. It was the design of W. F. Woodington, 1869. Approach it by the stadium entrance on the left, near the top of Anerley Hill.

Something of the gigantic scale of Paxton's masterpiece flowed into the decorations in its grounds in 1854. Of brick and iron covered with stucco, constructions by Waterhouse Hawkins supervised by Professor Richard Owen, **prehistoric monsters** were scattered in the surrounding park. In 1853 a high-spirited dinner party for twenty had been held in the partly completed iguanodon with Professor Owen in the chairman's seat — in the skull. 29 of the monsters survive on the islands in the lake at the southern end of the grounds. They were, and remain, a great feature. Joining this group on all fours is a statue of **Guy the Gorilla** by David Wynne (1962). Guy, perhaps the most popular animal of all time in the London Zoo, travelled from the French Cameroons to Paris, then to Regent's Park when he was about two years old. He died in 1978, aged 32.

One of the most successful of London's numerous statues of **Edward VII** (1841-1910) stands robed and bareheaded in Tooting Broadway. It is by L. Roselieb. Poor Edward was handicapped as Prince of Wales by his mother's refusal to allow him any role in matters of state, but when he succeeded to the throne (at the age of 59 and a grandfather) he proved her completely wrong. An extremely intelligent man, he had long been forced to seek occupation in the trivial but he quickly showed that he could deal adroitly with state business, particularly foreign affairs. He travelled widely and earned the nickname 'Edward the Peacemaker'. The *Entente Cordiale* with France was a major achievement. The public admired his interest in racing and yachting (he was the first reigning monarch to win the Derby) and even the colourful rumours about his amours only added to his popularity. He married Princess Alexandra of Denmark; they had six children, one of whom succeeded him as George V.

Lambeth's largest open space, Brockwell Park, has a drinking fountain to **Thomas Lynn Bristow**, MP for Norwood from 1885 to 1892, who led the campaign for the creation of the park but died during the opening ceremony, on Whit Monday, 1892.

Sir Henry Tate (1819-99) made a fortune in sugar refining, particularly, it is said, by the invention of sugar lumps. His plinth correctly describes him as 'an upright merchant, wise philanthropist'. As well as Liverpool University Library, and the Tate Gallery on Millbank, Sir Henry funded the public library before which his bronze bust by Sir Thomas Brock RA stands (1905), at the bottom of Brixton Hill.

At Brixton station, British Rail, with rare imagination, have set up statues of **three typical passengers**. The subjects, Peter Lloyd, Joy Battick and Karen Heistermann, were all volunteers; one signed on at the station and two at a local community centre. The statues, unveiled in 1986, are the work of Kevin Atherton.

East of Brixton at Denmark Hill the statues of **William Booth** (1829-1912), founder and first general of the Salvation Army, and his wife **Catherine Booth** (1829-90), stand outside the William Booth Memorial Officers' Training College at Champion Park. By G. E. Wade, they show the Booths in Army uniform, as if preaching. Booth began his first important evangelical work at Mile End Waste in the East End in 1861, aimed at converting the poor and outcast. It was not easy; there was ridicule and persecution but with the introduction of the name 'Salvation Army' in 1878, brass bands and a smart military-style uniform, a great expansion of the movement occurred. The magazine *War Cry* carried the message.

Booth knew that brutal living conditions and extreme poverty led to sin and the Army's spiritual ministrations were accompanied by social programmes, soup kitchens, cheap food shops, hostels, housing, legal aid and model factories. Booth's views were expressed in *In Darkest England and the Way Out* (1890) and other writings. He worked until he was 83, travelling and preaching (as Wesley had done), carrying the gospel to those otherwise untouched by religion. Like Wesley he found friends in high places and met crowned heads, including Edward VII. His work was continued by his eldest son Bramwell and his daughter Evangeline. The Salvation Army enjoys the affectionate nickname 'Sally Ann'.

Opposite the college is Ruskin Park. **Felix Mendelssohn-Bartholdy** (1809-47) paid a

number of visits to England. During one visit he composed his 'Spring Song' while staying in Denmark Hill in 1842 and a sundial in the park (which was named after John Ruskin, the art critic, who lived nearby) records this fact. It dates from the opening of the park in 1907.

North of Ruskin Park, in the courtyard of King's College Hospital at Denmark Hill, is

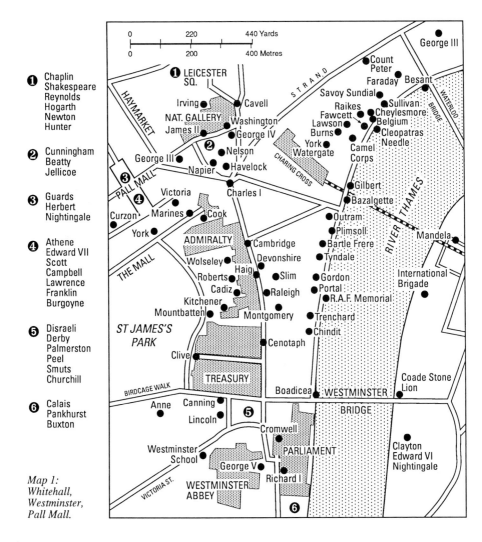

Map 1: Whitehall, Westminster, Pall Mall.

a statue by Matthew Noble (1862) to **Dr Robert Bentley Todd**, an Irishman, physician, and one of the founders of the hospital in 1839, when it was situated in Portugal Street, off the Strand. When the hospital moved to Denmark Hill the statue came too.

Camberwell New Road leads north-west from Denmark Hill to Kennington, where it is time to close the gates on our selection of London statues and monuments: but they are very special gates — at The Oval, headquarters of the Surrey County Cricket Club, a memorial to the great **Sir Jack Hobbs** (1882-1963), the Surrey and England cricketer, who at the time of his retirement in 1935 had the highest score ever achieved in first-class cricket, 61,221 runs and 197 centuries.

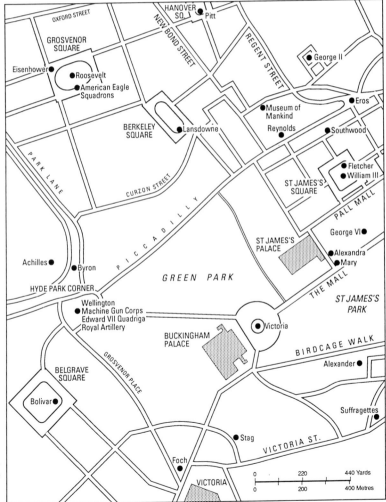

Map 2: Piccadilly, Hyde Park, Mayfair, Victoria.

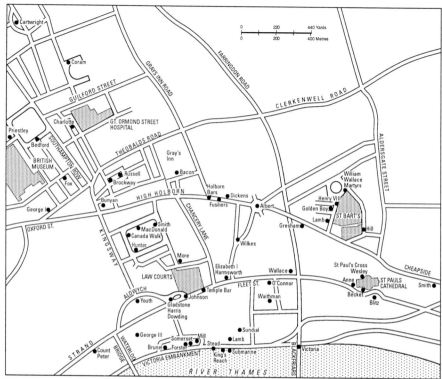

Map 3: Victoria Embankment, Holborn, St Paul's.

BIBLIOGRAPHY

Baker, Margaret. *Discovering London Statues and Monuments*. Shire, 1968 and 1980.

Blackwood, John. *London's Immortals: the Complete Outdoor Commemorative Statues*. Savoy, 1989.

Brown, F. B. *London Sculpture*. Pitman, 1934.

Byron, Arthur. *London Statues: a Guide to London's Outdoor Statues and Sculpture*. Constable, 1981.

Cooper, C. S. *The Outdoor Monuments of London*. Homeland Association Ltd, 1928.

Darke, J. *The Monument Guide to England and Wales*. Macdonald, 1991.

Gleichen, Lord Edward. *London's Open Air Statuary* . 1928.

Mannheim, F. J. *Lion Hunting in London*. Caducens Press, 1975.

Sitwell, Osbert. *The People's Album of London Statues*. Duckworth, 1928.

Thompson, Geoffrey. *London Statues*. Dent, 1971.

White, P. W. *On Public View: London's Open Air Sculpture*. Hutchinson, 1971.

INDEX

Page numbers in italic refer to illustrations.